Talking
about
GOD

OTHER BOOKS
BY DANIEL F. POLISH, PHD

*Bringing the Psalms to Life: How to Understand and
Use the Book of Psalms*
*Keeping Faith with the Psalms: Deepen Your
Relationship with God Using the Book of Psalms*

ABOUT THE
CENTER FOR RELIGIOUS INQUIRY SERIES

The Center for Religious Inquiry Series explores topics of religion and spirituality in an effort to develop new understandings of the various faith traditions. Each book will be developed in conjunction with the acclaimed Center for Religious Inquiry of St. Bartholomew's Church in New York City, a model for religious exploration across traditional religious lines that is being replicated in other cities across the United States.

The Center for Religious Inquiry Series

Exploring
the Meaning
of Religious
Life with
**Kierkegaard,
Buber,
Tillich** and
Heschel

Talking
about
GOD

Daniel F. Polish, PhD

Walking Together, Finding the Way®
SKYLIGHT PATHS®
PUBLISHING
Woodstock, Vermont

Talking about God:
Exploring the Meaning of Religious Life with Kierkegaard, Buber, Tillich and Heschel

2007 First Printing
© 2007 by Daniel F. Polish

Library of Congress Cataloging-in-Publication Data
Polish, Daniel F.
Talking about God : exploring the meaning of religious life with Kierkegaard, Buber, Tillich and Heschel / Daniel F. Polish.
    p. cm.
Includes bibliographical references.
ISBN-13: 978-1-59473-230-0 (hardcover)
ISBN-10: 1-59473-230-2 (hardcover)
1. Judaism—Essence, genius, nature. 2. Christianity—Essence, genius, nature. 3. Kierkegaard, Søren, 1813–1855. 4. Buber, Martin, 1878–1965. 5. Tillich, Paul, 1886–1965. 6. Heschel, Abraham Joshua, 1907–1972. 7. Abraham (Biblical patriarch) 8. Existentialism. I. Title.

BL53.P57 2007
204—dc22

2007029261

10 9 8 7 6 5 4 3 2 1
Manufactured in the United States of America
❀ Printed on recycled paper.
Cover Design: Tim Holtz
Cover and Title Page Art: *Sacrifice of Isaac,* by Lorenzo Ghiberti. Photo by James Hull.

SkyLight Paths Publishing is creating a place where people of different spiritual traditions come together for challenge and inspiration, a place where we can help each other understand the mystery that lies at the heart of our existence.
SkyLight Paths sees both believers and seekers as a community that increasingly transcends traditional boundaries of religion and denomination—people wanting to learn from each other, *walking together, finding the way.*

SkyLight Paths, "Walking Together, Finding the Way" and colophon are trademarks of LongHill Partners, Inc., registered in the U.S. Patent and Trademark Office.

Walking Together, Finding the Way®
Published by SkyLight Paths Publishing
A Division of LongHill Partners, Inc.
Sunset Farm Offices, Route 4, P.O. Box 237
Woodstock, VT 05091
Tel: (802) 457-4000   Fax: (802) 457-4004
www.skylightpaths.com

For the next generations
May God bless you and keep you

Leah

So unlike her biblical namesake in every way

And for

Noa
Talia
David

A blessing from out of Zion ...
To see your children's children
Shalom al Yisrael

CONTENTS

PREFACE

Living in an Age of Dialogue

We live in an age of dialogue. Within many of our own life-times the world has truly become the proverbial "global village." Thanks to the Internet, satellite phones, and other technological marvels, we can speak with whomever we want whenever we want, whether they are around the world or in our own neighborhood. And there is no limit to *what* we can talk about. Dialogue never ends.

In the world of religion our age is characterized by dialogue as well. It hasn't always been that way. For most of history people lived in more or less isolated homogeneous groups in which all members spoke the same language and subscribed to the tenets of the same religious tradition. They had little interaction with the outsiders who lived in proximity to them, and none with people who lived in other parts of the world. Religiously, that was the pattern that persisted until virtually the end of the twentieth century.

A NEW RELIGIOUS MOMENT

How dramatically different this present moment in religious life is, at least for Jews and Christians. Relations between

Jews and Christians were transformed radically in the fall of 1965 when the Roman Catholic Church issued the momentous document called *Nostra Aetate* (literally "In Our Time") at the end of the Second Vatican Council (Vatican II), which abolished the two-thousand-year-old charge that the Jews were a deicide people, annulled the teaching of contempt, and abrogated the notion that Christianity had, somehow, superseded Judaism as a valid expression of religious faith. In sum, it made the idea that Jews have a valid and legitimate way of relating to God part of official Catholic doctrine. It is impossible to overstate the significance of this document—indeed its publication might have been one of the most singular moments in religious history. Not only did it mandate a radically new understanding of Judaism, but by revising such a central Catholic teaching it also altered the way the Catholic Church thinks about itself. With Vatican II the relationship of Judaism and the Catholic Church and, in its wake, much of the rest of the Christian world was utterly redefined. A formerly destructive and hostile state of enmity was transformed into a relationship of respect, mutuality, and collaboration.

True, this relationship was made on earth and not in heaven, and like all relationships there have been, and will continue to be, different stages and moods. At times things will progress harmoniously and at other times experience setbacks. Things said by this Jewish leader or that Pope will cause consternation, and may even be read to suggest that the relationship is unraveling. But the fundamentals of this relationship are firm—because they are, ultimately, of such consequence to both parties. Whatever the tempest of any particular moment, the relationship of the Catholic Church and the Jewish people was irrevocably changed in 1965.

Just one seemingly trivial example of this new relationship: today we take it for granted that when a Jewish child becomes a bar or bat mitzvah, his or her school friends of any religion will be invited. But if such a thing happened before 1965 it was remarkable enough to provoke comment. In fact, Catholics who wanted to attend a Jewish service were required to seek a special dispensation from their priest— requests that were more often than not denied. Today it is a commonplace. Indeed it is so common that we read about Christian churches that feel compelled to create some kind of analogous event for their own thirteen-year-olds, who are demanding a bar mitzvah–type experience for themselves. Talk about dialogue.

More significantly, when Pope John Paul II visited the Great Synagogue of Rome on April 13, 1986, he shattered a millennia-old pattern. He was, as far as historians can ascertain, the first pope since Peter to set foot in a Jewish house of worship. When his successor, Pope Benedict, made his first trip abroad soon after he was elevated to the papacy, one of his first stops was a visit to a synagogue. The symbolism of such a visit is overwhelming. For two millennia the pope presided over a religion whose official stance toward Judaism was one of unmitigated contempt; today its watchword is "reconciliation." The Catholic Church even uses the Hebrew term for repentance, *teshuvah,* to describe the change in its orientation toward the Jews.

Representative of our new religious atmosphere are the many forums for interfaith conversation. In every possible configuration and at every level, Jews and Christians meet to get to know each other better and to explore the reality and meaning of living in such proximity to one another. Yet too often such gatherings seem unable to progress beyond well-intentioned pleasantries and the most superficial generalities ("We all believe in the same God, don't we?"). As well-intentioned as they might be, as generous in spirit and good faith, too many of our interfaith dialogues lack substance and challenging content.

It would be wonderful if more groups could come together to discuss subjects of real substance. Imagine how enriching it would be if Jews and Christians could come together to grapple with the writings of some of the recent great thinkers of both faiths, to plumb the depths of their differences and explore what they have in common. Participants on both sides would come away from such encounters with enlarged perspectives on their own and their opposite numbers' traditions. Such dialogues do more than foster transient good feelings—they create the potential for a genuinely fruitful relationship; they make it possible for us to find what unites us at the most profound levels.

It is my hope that this book can provide one resource for such substantive conversations. In it we will examine the writings of four authors, two each from the Jewish and Christian traditions: Martin Buber, Abraham Joshua Heschel, Søren Kierkegaard, and Paul Tillich. Though none of these thinkers is representative of the mainstream of his respective tradition or in any way speaks for the full spectrum of his community, each of them presents provocative and compelling insights, with implications that can stimulate meaningful and challenging conversation between people of various religious backgrounds and orientations.

I confess that my initial impulse in choosing these particular thinkers was entirely personal. They are writers I have read and studied for many years. They have challenged me in significant ways and moved me to explore new ways of understanding the phenomenon of faith in general and in my own tradition in particular. As I have returned to them over the years, I have consistently discovered new things. I have been fortunate to have the opportunity to teach modern religious thought in a wide variety of settings with all manner of students. And it has always been these four thinkers who have evoked the most discussion, inspiring students to view their own faiths with new eyes and to explore the faith traditions of their fellow students with open hearts and minds.

My choice of these four thinkers was reinforced by the recognition that they occupy a special place in modern religious thought. Each was remarkably prolific as well as provocative. Each has been studied by technical theologians and avidly read by the general public. Each has pioneered a seminal way of understanding the phenomenon of religion and, remarkably, has even contributed his own catchwords to the intellectual vocabulary of the larger public: Kierkegaard's "leap of faith"; Buber's "I and Thou"; Tillich's "ultimate concern"; and Heschel's "God in search of man."

As I set about outlining this project, I was struck as I had not been before by the interconnections between these four thinkers and the interplay, both personal and intellectual, that we find among them. Considered collectively, their ideas form a kind of mosaic. While they are not monolithic in their thought, we can find in their work a common pattern of insight that is especially helpful to us as we respond to the challenge of speaking to one another across the boundary lines of our various communities of faith. They share a unique willingness to express the ancient teachings of their respective traditions in the language of a more contemporary idiom. They share a recognition of the limitations of the finite human mind and human language in comprehending the fullness and grandeur of the Holy One while, at the same time, maintaining God's place at the center of the religious enterprise.

Perhaps most important for this book, these four thinkers offer a special opportunity for interfaith conversation. By locating the essence of their thought in the personal, rather than the doctrinal, the experiential rather than the received elements of their traditions, they speak to people of all religious backgrounds. And they offer us the opportunity to recognize the experience of religion that joins us, rather than the trappings of our respective traditions that may divide us. In this way, these four are especially appropriate for us to explore in shared study as we struggle to understand our own faith in the presence of the very different faith commitments of our neighbors.

I would add that I present these men as religious thinkers, not exemplars. Each of them was fully human in his fallibilities. In some circles those human limitations have placed their writings out of bounds. But I believe that the thought and insights of each of these men, flawed as they might be, have a worth and purpose beyond the limitations of the people who expounded them.

Needless to say, the brief sketches presented here do not pretend to be definitive or exhaustive in any way. It is my hope that, having provided grist for the mill of meaningful dialogical conversations, these intellectual hors d'oeuvres will whet your appetite for reading the works of any one (or all) of these thinkers on your own as you continue to wrestle with the profound questions and struggles that constitute all of our religious lives.

ACKNOWLEDGMENTS

I have incurred a tremendous debt to the many teachers with whom I have studied this material in so many settings, and whose inspiration is reflected in my own eagerness to engage with it once more. I regret that I did not take the opportunity to express my gratitude at the time. I do so now through my efforts to distill what I have learned from them and pass it on. Needless to add, all the errors and deficiencies in this book cannot be laid at their feet; whatever flaws it has are entirely attributable to me.

I also wish to express my gratitude:

To my wife, Gail, for allowing—no, really encouraging me—to steal time from our life together to work on this project.

To our daughter, Leah, who showed as much interest in modern religious thinkers as any seven-year-old can muster and who took real interest in following this project—even though it kept me from playing with her, and wanting to know, especially, how many pages Abba had left before he was finished.

To my sons, Jonathan and Ari—and to Lisa—who expressed amazement that I was at it again and who have listened over the years as the insights of these thinkers were refracted through my own teaching.

To my friend, Leonard Schoolman, whose idea it was in the first place that I should put onto the page a course that I had offered under his auspices at the Center for Religious Inquiry at St. Bartholomew's Church in New York City.

To the remarkable group of people at SkyLight Paths who made the editorial phase of this book such a pleasure: To Stuart M. Matlins for his friendship and enthusiastic support over the years; Emily Wichland for her insightful and gentle guidance; Arthur Goldwag for his close reading and creative suggestions as the text moved to its final form; and to Sarah McBride for holding it all together and moving it forward so expeditiously and with such consideration.

And finally, to my students in such a wide variety of settings who continually spark new questions in my reading of these thinkers, and who have kept my joy in the material fresh.

INTRODUCTION
Thinking Religiously

What do we mean by "religious thought"? Despite fairly widespread misperceptions to the contrary, religion is not the same thing as philosophy. That is, it is not exclusively a matter of understanding. Most of the time our religious identity is tied up in how we live our lives, the rituals we engage in, the holidays we celebrate, and the ways we comport ourselves in the world. Most religious people are not theologians; they are content to live with a less than complete understanding of the ideas or doctrines associated with their faith tradition. But sooner or later most of us come to a point when we wish to have a deeper understanding of the religious way of life we participate in. As often as not, this curiosity is stimulated by the need to justify or explain our faiths to others. Those are the times we turn to the expertise of religious thinkers whose role it is to take the religious tradition we are part of and "make sense" of it, for ourselves and others.

WHY BOTHER WITH
RELIGIOUS THOUGHT?

As citizens of a global village we regularly encounter people of different religious backgrounds than our own. They are our neighbors, our friends, perhaps even members of our extended families. We encounter different religious traditions in the news reports that stream into our homes, on the streets of our cities, and in our schools and places of work. Often something about those other religious traditions piques our curiosity, or becomes essential to making sense of an event in our world. At these times, too, we need the expertise of religious thinkers to help us understand the teachings of religious traditions other than our own.

None of us can be full participants in our own traditions or be fully informed members of our new planetary society without a deeper understanding of the contents of our various traditions. It may even be that to live a fully engaged human life, we need to devote time to understanding what the very phenomenon of "religion" itself is all about. This, too, is the stuff of religious thought. The thinkers whose work makes up the heart of this book are among the most respected, insightful, and challenging practitioners of their craft in modern times. Their teachings can help us understand ourselves and each other with greater depth and empathy. They inspire us to ponder questions that enlarge all of our intellectual and spiritual horizons.

WHAT MAKES MODERN RELIGIOUS THOUGHT MODERN?

What do we mean when we use the adjective "modern" to describe the works of Kierkegaard, Tillich, Heschel, and Buber? It is not merely a statement about chronology but of attitude. In what way does their work differ from work that we might call pre-modern or traditional? Of the many differences we could enumerate, we will limit ourselves to four.

The most striking thing about these authors is their self-conscious awareness that they are addressing people who do not necessarily share their beliefs. Traditional theology is addressed to believers; it explicates the faith system that is already acknowledged as true. The modern religious thinker writes with the knowledge that he or she will be read by people whose religious perspectives will be very different from his or her own. The reader might belong to an altogether different religious tradition, or be part of the same tradition but hold radically different perspectives. And in the contemporary age, unlike the ages that preceded it, the reader could be a person of no religious faith whatever. Whatever a modern religious thinker writes must make sense to people who do not share all of his or her assumptions.

These authors cannot make their case by what we would call an appeal to accepted authority. In pre-modern theology, writers often cite scripture or some other source that is universally accepted by the members of that tradition and have that "proof-text" establish or affirm the correctness of their opinion. Indeed in both Jewish and Christian traditions, one of the most common forms of religious discussion is commentary on a text that is accepted by that faith community as sacred. In the modern pluralistic setting in which our four authors wrote, such an appeal to authority or canon would not be, in itself, at all persuasive. Thus none of these thinkers takes recourse to that line of reasoning. Accepted tradition, practice, or understanding does not provide a sufficient foundation for their arguments.

Traditional religious discussion tends to be self-referential, that is, it explains itself circularly, in the terms of that tradition itself. In contrast, our four thinkers seek to explain themselves in terms that will be comprehensible to all readers, whether members of the author's tradition or not. Indeed a primary, self-conscious goal of each of these thinkers is to express his religious insights in the language of the general culture rather than in the idiom of the insular faith community.

A final, and perhaps the most significant, characteristic of modern religious thinking is that it is individualistic. While traditionally people's religious identity has been mediated or determined by their membership in this group or that (often an accident of birth or geography), modern religious thought addresses itself to individuals as self-determining free agents in their religious lives. To the extent that there is any desire to persuade, none of these authors seeks to entice his readers to join any particular group or abandon their affiliation; rather, they seek to persuade their readers to interrogate their own accustomed ways of understanding some fundamental religious issue or set of issues, to wrap their minds around something new and challenging.

WHAT DO WE MEAN BY "EXISTENTIALIST"?

All four thinkers can be properly characterized as "existential"—for all their differences, it is one thing they undoubtedly hold in common. But what does that mean? *Existentialism* is one of those words that, when used in personal conversation, causes people's eyes to glaze over. In more technical settings it tends to elude definition. But in the sense that I make use of it here, it implies the idea that, as Shakespeare put it long ago, "there are more things in heaven and earth ... than are dreamt in your philosophy."

Existentialist thought recognizes that in our everyday lives we make most of our decisions not exclusively on the basis of reason or rationality, but in significant measure on the basis of things we cannot begin to express (or sometimes even acknowledge) in rational terms. In trying to make sense of the human situation, philosophical discussion cannot depend exclusively on reason but must take these noncognitive elements into consideration as well. Many of the things we consider most important in life—many of our most profound values and beliefs—resist being reduced to simple logical propositions. All four of these thinkers share the awareness that elements of what they wish to convey will necessarily elude their ability to express them. This is precisely what allows us to characterize them all as existentialists. In their treatment of religious issues, each was disposed to give credence to what we might call intuition—perceptions that are not inherently rational. Each gave primacy to experience over understanding, and each, at times, expressed antipathy to the rigid categories of logical thought.

LINES OF CONNECTION

So our "quartet" of thinkers may all properly be described as modern. They are also, to varying degrees, existentialist. They share other significant commonalities as well, some intellectual and some even touching on their personal histories.

Of the four thinkers presented here, Søren Kierkegaard, appropriately, stands alone. I say "appropriately" because, as we shall see, he is very much an exponent of solitude. Unlike the others, who were more engaged with the realities of the world around them, Kierkegaard virtually withdrew from human contact and devoted himself with an almost monastic devotion to speculation and writing. Despite this, his impact on the wider world beyond his study has been immense. The span of his life, 1813 to 1855, sets him half a century earlier than the other three, but he is inextricably bound up with them because his work exerted such a profound influence over each of them. Tillich referred to Kierkegaard often in his own work. In *The Courage to Be,* Tillich describes the origins of existentialism:

> When Kierkegaard broke away from Hegel's system
> of essences he did two things: he proclaimed an exis-

tential attitude and he instigated a philosophy of existence. He realized that the knowledge of that which concerns us infinitely is possible only in an attitude of infinite concern, in an existential attitude. (p. 125)

Tillich might have added that he, too, was a proponent of this understanding. As scholar Michael Novack has noted, "Tillich thought of himself as continuing the tradition of Kierkegaard's infinite passion and interest."

In a powerful analysis of Kierkegaard's *Fear and Trembling,* Buber noted:

The first book of Kierkegaard's that I read as a young man was *Fear and Trembling,* which is built entirely upon the Biblical narrative of the sacrifice of Isaac. I still think of that hour to-day because it was then that I received the impulse to reflect upon the categories of the ethical and the religious in their relation to each other. (*The Eclipse of God,* p. 115)

Buber acknowledges his admiration of Kierkegaard's project and, by implication, his indebtedness to it, but he nonetheless takes issue with Kierkegaard's idea of the "teleological suspension of the ethical." We will have more to say about this in a later chapter.

Heschel's last book, *A Passion for Truth,* compared Kierkegaard to one of the great Hasidic masters, Menachem Mendl of Kotzk, called the Kotzker, whom Heschel regards as one of his own formative teachers. Heschel writes:

> When, long ago, I began to read the works of
> Kierkegaard, the father of modern existentialism, I
> was surprised to find that many of his thoughts were
> familiar to me. I realized that a number of his perspec-
> tives and basic concerns had reached me from the
> teachings of the Kotzker. (p. 85)

He goes on to note, "Theologically—in dogma and ritual—
the Kotzker and Kierkegaard were worlds apart," but then
he proceeds to take note of the fact that is most salient for
him:

> Yet, though their points of departure and their con-
> texts were basically different, the problems they con-
> fronted on the level of living their commitment, on
> the level of *depth-theology*, were often the same....
> How does one exercise one's ultimate commitment?
> (p. 86)

Heschel could well have added that those same qualities
were characteristic of his own work and his own life.
Following his own theological algebra, Heschel, by identify-
ing himself as a follower of the Kotzker, was at the same time
proclaiming himself a disciple of Kierkegaard. Not that
Heschel always agreed with the earlier thinker. In the end,
he, like Buber, would take issue with Kierkegaard's notion
that absolute devotion to God can ever necessitate a radical
opposition to the laws of justice. But whether in agreement
or disagreement, it is noteworthy that Heschel, even at the
end of his career and his life, continued to be engaged in con-

versation with the Kierkegaard who so inspired him in his younger years.

Kierkegaard left a profound imprint on the thinking of all three of the younger members of our quartet. But their common indebtedness to the earlier thinker was only one of the things this cohort had in common. Though they came from markedly different backgrounds in central and eastern Europe, each of them was a product of the intellectual ferment of early-twentieth-century Germany, and all of them fled the barbarity into which that nation descended. Heschel and Tillich made their way to the United States, while Buber went to the emerging Jewish settlement in the British colony that was then called Palestine.

It is a little-appreciated fact that Buber and Tillich shared a long personal history. David Novak relates this telling anecdote:

> On the personal level, the relationship between the older Buber and the younger Tillich is best illustrated by the following story that I heard from someone who was in attendance at a lecture Buber delivered at Union Theological Seminary in New York in 1952, during his first visit to America, a visit in which he made a profound impression on American intellectual circles. At the end of the lecture, Buber indicated that he would entertain questions from the audience. From the back of the crowded lecture hall, Paul Tillich arose and quite respectfully (as was his usual manner) addressed a rather complicated question to Buber. According to my reliable informant, Buber

looked up from his text and said, "Ah, Paulus, it is you."
Then he walked down the aisle and stood directly in
front of Tillich, who was considerably taller than he,
raised his index finger up at Tillich's startled face and
said, "Paulus, Paulus, you asked me the same question
in Germany thirty years ago. Don't you remember
what I answered you then?!" ("Buber and Tillich," pp.
159–160)

Tillich also specifically cites Buber throughout his work, which is often imbued with Buberian ideas, though the two were not always in agreement.

Buber and Heschel, too, had a long association. In 1935, when Heschel, at age twenty-seven, was at the beginning of his career and the fifty-two-year-old Buber was already well known, Heschel made a deliberate effort to establish himself in the older man's regard. The two would become close collaborators. When Heschel had completed his doctoral studies in Berlin, Buber invited him to teach a program of adult Jewish study at the legendary Judisches Lehrhaus in Frankfurt, which he had established with his friend and colleague Franz Rosenzweig. "Buber gave me my first job," Heschel said later. In 1937, as Buber prepared to leave Frankfurt to emigrate to Palestine, Heschel had an opportunity to reciprocate when he tutored his mentor in modern, spoken Hebrew. When Buber finally left Germany, he appointed Heschel to serve as his successor as director of the Lehrhaus and of the Central Organization for Adult Jewish Education.

A record of the centuries-long rabbinical "conversation" that established the forms and patterns of Jewish religious practice, the Talmud is a multivolume text whose authority in Jewish tradition is second only to the Bible. Buber was antagonistic to the external forms of religion—it was ideas and concepts that moved him. So he never owned a set of the Talmud—that is, not until he was presented with one as a gift by Heschel on his sixtieth birthday. (Buber is said to have thanked him by saying, "I've always wanted one.") From the beginning, Heschel developed his own thought in reference to, and often in opposition to, that of the older man. The connection continued throughout their lives.

As for the third leg of this triangle, the relationship seems not to have been as warm. Heschel and Tillich were acquainted with one another and frequently presented learned papers at the same conferences. Heschel was also close friends with Tillich's famous colleague at Union Theological Seminary, Reinhold Neibuhr. But Heschel and Tillich's relationship seems to have been more intellectual and collegial than personal. Heschel makes use of one of Tillich's well-known catchphrases (religion as our "ultimate concern") in *Man's Quest for God*, yet he does not attribute it to Tillich and, even more significantly—either playfully or for rhetorical purpose—he employs it in a wholly different fashion than Tillich did. This indirect, slighting allusion to Tillich is emblematic of the relationship between two men who occupied much of the same terrain without having more than glancing personal interactions. Still, their intellectual relationship is significant, and that is our primary concern. As we shall see, their perspectives often converged and at times played off of one another. We shall see them arrive at significantly similar conclusions from very different directions. And we shall note where their divergences underscore what is most distinctive about each of them.

The three later thinkers shared other qualities as well. In contrast to Kierkegaard, all of them were personally involved in the political and social issues of their time. Buber and Tillich were active participants in the German religious socialist movement in the years following World War I. Upon arriving in Palestine, Buber threw himself into activities aimed at establishing a binational state of Arabs and Jews. Heschel achieved his greatest public recognition for his extensive involvement in the civil rights movement of the 1960s and later for his activities opposing the Vietnam War. One of his last public appearances was as part of a delegation at the Danbury, Connecticut, penitentiary to celebrate the release of the Catholic priest and anti-Vietnam war activist Daniel Berrigan.

As existentialist thinkers, Buber, Tillich, and Heschel shared the understanding that thought in itself was not the highest good—of much greater importance was how convictions were translated into action. Each of them engaged with the realities of their world, lived out the ideas they espoused, and taught with their lives no less than with their words. In this way they became not just theoreticians of religion but also practitioners of their most significant commitments.

EXPRESSING TRADITIONAL IDEAS
IN MODERN TERMS

The qualities that we have earlier identified as characterizing modern religious thought are all present in the work of

Buber, Tillich, and Heschel. All of them expressed religious
ideas in terms that were accessible to people who were not of
their own religious background, and, more pointedly, to secular people who had no religious commitment at all. Tillich
has written, "My whole theological work has been directed
to the interpretation of religious symbols in such a way that
the secular man—and we all are secular—can understand
and be moved by them" (Brown, p. 88). Elsewhere, Mark
Kline Taylor notes, "Tillich ... presented a theological
'method of correlation' by which essential symbols of
Christian tradition could be correlated with human being
and existence" (Taylor, p. 22).

Buber has said that his studies of Hasidism, the Jewish
tradition of applied mysticism, were the soil out of which his
later I-Thou philosophy of dialogic encounter grew. But that
body of work is written in such a way that unless you knew
of its lineage, you would not connect this profound teaching
to its roots in the Jewish religious tradition. If Buber's
thought is Hasidic, it is presented in a thoroughly secular
(some would say "denatured") way. Still, Buber and his
interpreters insisted on the connection. The link between
Buber's involvement with Hasidism and his concern for the
general human condition is made explicit in an anthology of
his writings titled *Hasidism and Modern Man*. Maurice
Friedman, perhaps the leading interpreter of Buber's thought
and the author of his definitive biography, writes that:

> Hasidism played a central role both in the develop-
> ment of Buber's interpretation of Judaism and in the
> evolution of his general philosophy, and perhaps

even more than the Bible, it served as the meeting point between the two.... Hasidism was uniquely qualified to lend impetus and solid content to the progression of Buber's thought from his early period of mysticism through his middle period of religious existentialism to his mature philosophy of dialogue, or the "I-Thou" relation. (cited in Noveck, pp. 188–89)

Walter Kaufmann, in the prologue to his translation of Buber's *I and Thou*, asserts:

This book ... speaks to those who no longer believe.... The book is steeped in Judaism.... In fact, *Ich und Du* is one of the great documents of Jewish faith. (pp. 32, 35)

But we would not necessarily know that by reading it because Buber's language is so universal. In a similar vein, Franklin Sherman has noted of Heschel:

In 1951 there appeared Heschel's study entitled *The Sabbath: Its Meaning for Modern Man*. Note both the title and the subtitle in this case. The Sabbath, a venerable Jewish observance, is to be interpreted in terms of "its meaning for modern man"—a typical Heschel enterprise, linking an ancient heritage with the modern situation. (p. 19)

Each of these thinkers sought to express the ideas and symbols of his respective tradition in language that could be apprehended by those who were not members of that tradition, and in terms that had a universal relevance.

RELIGIOUS DIALOGUE: ENCOUNTER WITH THE OTHER

Buber, Heschel, and Tillich also shared an involvement with the project of dialogue among religious traditions that is unique to the modern age. Buber wrote extensively about Jewish and Christian issues and pursued opportunities to engage in mutual exploration with all manner of Christian thinkers, as exemplified by his decades-long "encounter" with Tillich. He also includes references to the religious traditions of the East throughout his work. In his latter years he was deeply involved in conversations with Japanese Zen Buddhist Roshis. Tillich, as well, developed a deep fascination toward the end of his life with the study of the religious diversity of humankind and, like Buber, began to immerse himself in the study of Eastern religious traditions and to incorporate the insights he gleaned from those encounters into his thought.

Heschel made remarkable contributions to Jewish-Christian dialogue. As would be expected for someone as passionately involved as he was in the civil rights movement, he developed deep bonds with Rev. Martin Luther King Jr. Teaching at The Jewish Theological Seminary in New York City afforded him opportunities for significant interaction with the students and faculty of Union Theological Seminary, which was just across the street. Indeed he served for a period of time as visiting professor at that institution.

Perhaps his most enduring bond to that school was the close friendship he forged with its renowned faculty member, Reinhold Niebuhr.

But Heschel's most significant contribution to the building of bridges between Christians and Jews were his visits with Pope Paul VI in the midst of the Second Vatican Council, in which he was given the opportunity to represent Jewish perspectives and concerns. Initiated perhaps as merely symbolic gestures on the part of the Vatican, those visits resulted in the forging of close personal bonds between this Jewish scholar and thinker and the head of the Roman Catholic Church—something that would have been impossible to imagine in an earlier age.

The involvement of all three of these thinkers in interfaith dialogue and conversation are emblematic of all that makes their work unique to this moment in time and distinguishes their thought as being of special usefulness for Jews and Christians today as we seek to gain a deeper insight into each other's faith traditions—and our own.

ABRAHAM AS A WAY INTO MODERN RELIGIOUS THOUGHT

In deciding which selections from the works of these four thinkers to include in this book, I was intrigued by the possibility of building on the foundation laid by Kierkegaard by examining their ideas through the lens of their treatment of the Bible in general and the figure of the biblical patriarch Abraham in particular. Abraham provides the emotional and theological core of Kierkegaard's monumental *Fear and*

Trembling. Though Abraham figures to a lesser extent in the work of the other thinkers, the ways that each of them addresses him can nonetheless provide us with significant insights into the whole of their individual thought projects. In the pages of this book, Abraham serves as a connective thread that binds all four of these thinkers together. Indeed, from a different perspective, this book might be read as a kind of modern religio-philosophical commentary on that biblical patriarch.

It is altogether appropriate to focus on Abraham as we pursue the project of interfaith dialogue. Jews and Christians (and Muslims as well) regard Abraham as their spiritual father. It was Abraham who, according to the Book of Genesis, was the first to know the God of the biblical tradition. From a more modern vantage, we often refer to Abraham as the first monotheist. It was Abraham whose covenant with God forms the basis of biblical faith, which is regarded by Jews, Christians, and Muslims alike as finding its ultimate expression in their respective religious traditions.

Abraham is constantly invoked in the Jewish liturgy. Jews address the central prayer in the worship service to, "Our God, and God of our fathers, God of Abraham, God of Isaac and God of Jacob ... " This pattern was drawn from the practice of the Bible itself. When Isaac first encounters God, God tells him, "I am the God of your father, Abraham" (Gen. 26:24). And when Jacob, Isaac's own son, has his first encounter with God, God states, "I am the Lord, the God of your father Abraham and the God of Isaac" (Gen. 28:13).

And then, generations later, when Moses encounters God in the burning bush, God states, "I am the God of your father, the God of Abraham, the God of Isaac, and the God of Jacob" (Exod. 3:6). The unique symbol of the covenant established with Abraham, circumcision, serves as the basis of the birth rite of passage for Jewish boys, the *brit milah*, which is regarded as definitive of Jewish identity.

Turning to the Christian tradition, the Gospel of Matthew begins, "The book of the genealogy of Jesus Christ, the son of David, the son of Abraham. Abraham was the father of Isaac, and Isaac the father of Jacob ... " And so forth until we come to verse 15, which reads:

> ... and Matthan the father of Jacob and Jacob the father of Joseph the husband of Mary of whom Jesus was born, who is called the Christ. So all the generations from Abraham to David were fourteen generations, and from David to the deportation to Babylon fourteen generations, and from the deportation to Babylon to the Christ fourteen generations.

Later in Matthew, Jesus is depicted as saying, "Have you not read what was said to you by God, 'I am the God of Abraham, and the God of Isaac, and the God of Jacob ... '" (Matt. 22:31–32).

In Paul's Epistle to the Galatians a very different role for Abraham is suggested:

> So you see that it is men of faith [not merely those who have been circumcised and are entered into

Abraham's covenant, "in the flesh"] who are sons of Abraham. And the scripture, foreseeing that God would justify the gentiles by faith, preached the gospel beforehand to Abraham, saying, "in you shall all the nations of the earth be blessed." So then, those who are men of faith are blessed with Abraham who had faith. (Gal. 3:7–9).

To Paul, who was seeking to justify his preaching to gentiles as well as Jews, Abraham becomes the "father in faith" of all those who believe in God, gentile or Israelite, circumcised or not.

The figure of Abraham occupies a central role in both faith traditions. How religious thinkers view the figure of Abraham and employ that image in their own thought, then, is of no small value in revealing their fundamental outlook. We shall pay special attention to the treatment of Abraham in the passages selected from the extensive works of each of these thinkers as we examine them to gain insight into the major ideas, values, and themes that they articulate.

SØREN KIERKEGAARD
The Knight of Faith

The Danish thinker Søren Kierkegaard (1813–1855) would almost certainly have rejected the label most often applied to him a century and a half after his death: theologian. That he was what we would call God-intoxicated, he probably would not have denied. But being called a theologian might have caused him much amusement. As far as he was concerned, he was engaged in the project of understanding the human condition, exploring the way human beings ought to live their lives.

> That he was what we would call God-intoxicated, he probably would not have denied. But being called a theologian might have caused him much amusement.

Kierkegaard's writings are generally regarded as precursors of the philosophical approach we call existentialism. He rejected the then-dominant philosophy of Hegel, with its emphasis on abstractions and absolutes, and emphasized instead the individual and the ways the decisions a person makes determine his or her life. Repeatedly and consistently,

Kierkegaard emphasized human experience over rationalistic thought. Each of the questions he laid before us is ultimately answered by subjective, personal experience, not an abstract philosophical or theological system.

KIERKEGAARD'S UNIQUE
LITERARY STYLE

Kierkegaard was an exquisite writer. What he was not was a systematic thinker. Rather, he played with ideas, experimented with positions. Kierkegaard held up philosophical questions like so many exquisite jewels and turned them in the light, revealing new facets of whatever issue was at hand with each change of perspective. He offered no final resolution to the questions he laid before us, but rather suggested tentative, provisional positions—often in contradiction with one another—for us to explore ourselves. It is as if he invites us to try on a position and see whether it is appropriate. After we have immersed ourselves in one possible resolution of the problem, he invites us to try on another one ... and the next one after that. And so on through any particular piece of his writing—and indeed from one work to the next. His works were initially published under a variety of pseudonyms, as if to suggest, by the disparity of authorial attributions, the partial nature of the position or positions each posited. Kierkegaard offers us the opportunity, in artfully crafted prose, to experience what it would be like to live in this life stance or that one.

KIERKEGAARD AND THE LIMITS OF HUMAN UNDERSTANDING

For Kierkegaard the thinker, *the* central issue is his awareness of the limitation of his understanding; indeed, the necessary limitations of what anyone can understand—what Tillich would later come to characterize as the problem of human finitude. Unlike the classical philosophers and Hegel, Kierkegaard does not assume or pretend to assume that reason and logic can lead him to complete or final answers. Because he is human, and his understanding finite, absolute truth will inevitably escape him. All he can do is glimpse aspects of the truth and, as a teacher, help us experience them for ourselves. Though incomplete and necessarily partial, the insights he brings us to nevertheless exceed any approximation that we might come to on our own—or even the total of all the approximations we might experience over time.

Given this perspective, Kierkegaard as a religious thinker could hardly be expected to address the issue of the nature of God or to provide us with proof of God's existence. What he can and does discuss is the nature of the human relationship with God.

KIERKEGAARD'S LIFE AND THOUGHT

Appropriately for a thinker whose work focused so much on the experience of the subjective individual, Kierkegaard's life is of immense significance in understanding his intellectual work. The name Kierkegaard is the Danish equivalent of "graveyard," the cemetery that stood just outside the door of the church. From all accounts Kierkegaard was a rather grim and austere figure, well deserving of the name. Though raised in comfortable economic circumstances, his life does not seem to have been a happy or carefree one. His childhood was marked by solemnity and religious earnestness, qualities that remained with him for the rest of his life.

On the most profound personal level, Kierkegaard seems to have been incapable of coming to terms with the particularities of mortal, earthly life. One incident in particular finds itself refracted in his writings. When he was twenty-eight years old, he became engaged to a young woman of some social standing, Regine Olson. But soon afterward, despite his evident love for her, he cruelly broke the engagement in a way that he deliberately intended to reflect discredit upon himself. Thereafter he withdrew from the world and commenced a life of absolute seclusion, devoting himself wholly to his studies and his writing. Nonetheless he apparently continued to harbor the belief that, through some agency of fate, he would eventually be reunited with his beloved Regine. He maintained this wishful illusion until he inadvertently learned of her engagement, and then marriage, to another man.

This same pattern of ambivalent engagement with the realities of life in the world is reflected in his relations with the church. Although he had cherished the hope of receiving a position in the official Church of Denmark, when the opportunity was finally presented to him, he found himself incapable of accepting it. Soon thereafter his invectives against organized Christianity grew increasingly shrill as he denounced the church for the compromises it had made with the life of this earth.

Perhaps we might dismiss Kierkegaard as an unfortunately melancholic soul who was incapacitated by neurosis. But there is a profound connection between the vicissitudes of his life and his philosophical orientation. These episodes from his life reflect the acuteness with which he felt the fundamental divide that separates two aspects of reality. He was exquisitely, painfully aware of the tension between the infinite and absolute that is God and the limitations of the finite and temporal that characterize the realm of human experience. This tension determines the very literary form of his work and constitutes a theme to which he returns repeatedly in his writing.

THREE REALMS OF EXISTENCE

For Kierkegaard existence is divided into three realms that exist in perpetual tension. The first realm he calls the "aesthetic," though perhaps today we would use the term *hedonistic* to describe it. This is the realm of the temporal; those who inhabit it are completely devoted to personal pleasure and are dominated by their senses. The second realm Kierkegaard called the "ethical" (though from his description it seems clear that he was focused on the philosophical). A person whose life is lived in this realm does acknowledge a sphere beyond his or her own self-interest, which Kierkegaard characterized as "the impersonal ideal." This ideal is based on reason. We might hear in it echoes of the Hegelian philosophical approach that was dominant during Kierkegaard's lifetime.

The final realm is the one that Kierkegaard called "religious." The religious realm utterly transcended the aesthetic or sensual and the ethical or philosophical realms; it is totally divorced from the mundane concerns of everyday life. It is completely beyond what can be experienced in finite terms or conceived in rational or even abstract categories. To attain it no reason-based decision making is necessary or even possible. A person arrives there only by taking, in Kierkegaard's well-known phrase, a leap of faith.

We see in this schema the radical disjunction Kierkegaard makes between the things of this world and that which completely transcends it. There is no continuum, no gradual stages of ascent; just the two inalterably opposed existences. This break makes it impossible to discuss things in the realm of religion; all we can meaningfully talk about are matters of aesthetics or ethics. It is this bracketing of the issue of abstractions and absolutes, this exclusive focus on what can be known and experienced, that makes Kierkegaard a precursor of existentialism. And it is this same break, when conjoined with Kierkegaard's commitment to pursuing the realm of the religious, that made it impossible for him to commit to anything of the this-worldly, finite, utterly inferior realm—not his beloved Regine nor the church as it existed in his experience.

This schema is the cause of the great dilemma that Kierkegaard sought to address. Despite rejecting Hegel, Kierkegaard tended to see the world in dialectical terms (albeit without the ameliorating presence of Hegel's synthesis, which ultimately reconciled the two opposites). His world, as reflected in the title of one of Kierkegaard's books, was starkly understood in terms of either/or. Either you give yourself over wholly to the realm of the religious or you live a life dominated by the senses.

THE GREAT TENSION

In Kierkegaard's analysis of the human situation, all people live torn between the two poles of this irreconcilable dialectic. Our bodies—material, temporal—pull us toward the senses and the things of this earth. But we are composed of spirit as well. That spirit provides us with some intimation of that other realm. This awareness of the dichotomy between how we live and how we *should* be living fills us with angst—the German word for dread or terror. Angst summons us to separate ourselves from the things of this world. If we answer that summons, we experience redemption. If we do not, if we insist on remaining in the realm of the senses, we are doomed to despair.

There is a significant commonality in this dimension of Kierkegaard's teaching and the teachings of Siddartha Gautama, the Buddha/the Enlightened One of the Buddhist tradition. The Buddha regarded both the aesthetic/hedonistic—the realm of the senses—and the ethical/philosophical as maya/illusion. We choose to hold onto the things we experience on this side of the divide because we are deluded into imagining them to be the real, the highest we can aspire to, not realizing (or not accepting) that there is a greater good available to us if only we would release the shadows we have embraced. The Buddha urged us to let go of the things of this world so we could enter wholly into the realm of unmediated reality. This is what he meant by the achievement of nirvana/liberation. Casual readers of the teachings of either the Buddha or Kierkegaard might regard their messages as gloomy and pessimistic. But both understood themselves to be hopeful because they pointed out the way for us to transcend the limits of our temporal reality and invited us to grasp the infinite. They were life-denying only in the sense that they called us away from the lesser life of this incomplete, impermanent, and transient substitute for reality to the true and the real. The Buddha spoke of himself as being no abstract theoretician. Instead, he said he was like a doctor who made a diagnosis of the human condition and offered us a prescription for the remedy. No doubt Kierkegaard would have understood himself in these same terms.

KIERKEGAARD'S ABRAHAM: FEAR AND TREMBLING

One of Kierkegaard's towering masterpieces is *Fear and Trembling*, published in 1843. It is to this book that we will now turn. Since, in Kierkegaard's intellectual system, our human limitations make it impossible for us to talk meaningfully about the infinite per se, Kierkegaard limited his discussion to the human side of that divide. Thus *Fear and Trembling* is an extended examination of the nature of faith, expressed through various perspectives on the biblical story of the binding of Isaac. This story is immediately familiar to observant Jews because it is told in the Torah portion that is included in the religious service for Rosh Hashanah, the Jewish New Year. But for those who don't recall it, it is recounted in Genesis 22, which follows in its entirety:

> And it was after these things that God put Abraham to the test. And He said, "Take now your son, your only one, Isaac, whom you love and go to the land I will show you and offer him up as an offering on one of the mountains which I will tell you of." So Abraham got up early In the morning and saddled his donkey and took two of his servant lads with him, and Isaac his son. And he cut some wood for the offering and got up and went to the place that the Lord had told him of. It was on the third day, Abraham lifted up his eyes and saw the place from afar. And Abraham said to the servant lads, "You stay here with the donkey and I and the lad will go over there and we will worship and return to you." And Abraham took the wood for the offering and placed it on Isaac his son. And he took the fire[stone] and a knife in his hand, and the two of them continued on together. And Isaac said to Abraham, his father, "My father." And he answered, "Here I am, my son." And he said, "Here is the fire[stone] and here is the wood. But where is the lamb for the offering?" And Abraham said, "God will provide a lamb for the offering, my son." And the two of them continued on together.

And they came to the place that God had told them of and Abraham built there an altar, and arranged the wood, and bound Isaac, his son, and placed him on the altar upon the wood. And Abraham reached out his hand and took the knife to slaughter his son. And an angel of the Lord called out to him from the heavens and said, "Abraham, Abraham." And he said, "Here I am." And [the angel] said, "Do not reach out your hand toward the lad, and do not make even a mark upon him. For now I know that you revere God, seeing that you have not withheld your son, your only one, from me. And Abraham lifted up his eyes and saw, and behold a ram behind him caught by its horns in a thicket. And Abraham went and took the ram and offered it up as an offering in place of his son. And Abraham called the name of the place Adonai Yireh/the Lord's Vision. Thus it is said to this day, "On the mount of the Lord there is vision."

And the angel of the Lord called out to Abraham a second time from the heavens. And he said, "By Myself have I sworn, says the Lord, since you have done this thing and not withheld your son, your only one, I will surely bless you with blessing and cause the greatness of your descendants to be as great as the stars of the heavens and the sand that is on the shores of the sea. And your descendants shall take possession of the gates of their enemies. And by your descendants shall all the nations of the earth be blessed because you have listened to My voice." And

Abraham returned to his servant lads. And they got up and they went together to Beer Sheva. And Abraham dwelled in Beer Sheva.

Kierkegaard's interpretation of this story, which occupies such an important place in the biblical tradition, is deeply strange, unique, and surprising.

FEAR AND TREMBLING: THE BOOK

When *Fear and Trembling* was first published, Kierkegaard wrote in his journal:

> Oh, once I am dead, *Fear and Trembling* alone will be enough for an imperishable name as an author. Then it will be read, translated into foreign languages as well. The reader will almost shrink from the frightful pathos in the book. (Kierkegaard, *Journals*, vol.10)

Kierkegaard can be forgiven his immodesty. *Fear and Trembling* is as beautiful today and every bit as compelling and relevant as it must have been to his contemporaries. It is not an easy book to read, but if you can make your way through it, if you consider it carefully, it is like dining from a superb smorgasbord. So many things to choose from, and all so wonderful; so many exciting and important ideas to reflect on and explore! Here I will select only a few excerpts from the book to help us address some of its most significant themes. First, an encomium to Abraham:

> Abraham was great … great by reason of his power whose strength is impotence, great by reason of his wisdom whose secret is foolishness, great by reason of his hope whose form is madness, great by reason of the love which is hatred of oneself. (Kierkegaard, p. 31)

Kierkegaard delights in expressing himself through paradox. He sounds in no small measure like the teachings of the Chinese classic, the Tao Te Ching:

> The Tao/Way that can be told is not the true Tao/Way. Finite phenomena that you can name/comprehend are not real phenomena. (ch. 1)

And also

> The Sage acts by doing nothing
> Teaches without saying anything
> He has [things] but doesn't possess [them]. (ch. 2)

The Tao Te Ching, like the Zen tradition of Buddhism, uses paradox to shatter the categories of rational thought. True understanding for the Tao Te Ching, for Zen, and for Kierkegaard lies beyond the boundaries of the finite, limited human mind. True understanding pertains to what is infinite. Thus Kierkegaard will resort to paradoxical, seemingly non-sensical statements again and again to make his point.

For Kierkegaard, Abraham's greatness rests on his disengagement from the things of this world. He cannot be defined by the conventional categories of our everyday lives. Nor does he care to be. Call him impotent or foolish or mad—it does not concern him. The hope he holds onto is mad, at least mad in terms of our conventional modes of thought, in terms of our accepted categories of reason. But that is precisely what makes him great.

The ultimate expression of Abraham's greatness is the "love which is hatred of oneself." For Kierkegaard, love of God, of the infinite, is most powerfully expressed by self-denial—living without putting the wants or even the needs of oneself first, in fact in transcending our very attachment to ourself. In rejecting the finite and cleaving to the infinite, we abandon even our attachment to ourselves. It is this love that Kierkegaard finds expressed in hate, and this hatred constitutes the outlines of the faith that Abraham epitomizes. This faith inspires awe, even reverence, in Kierkegaard:

> Abraham I cannot understand, in a certain sense there is nothing I can learn from him but astonishment. If people fancy that by considering the *outcome* of this story they might be moved to believe, they deceive themselves and want to swindle God out of the first movement of faith, the infinite resignation. (Kierkegaard, p. 48)

Kierkegaard published *Fear and Trembling* under a pseudonym, Johannes de Silentio. Johannes, like Kierkegaard's other pseudonyms, was conceived of as a persona, a character in a drama. Kierkegaard endowed each of these purported authors with their own personal qualities. It is Johannes who fails to "understand" Abraham, not Kierkegaard. Still, the point that Kierkegaard makes by this ruse is crucial to his project. Those things that pertain to the other side of the great divide cannot be "understood" in the way that we conventionally make use of that term. Kierkegaard here subtly juxtaposes two primary modes of understanding: rational understanding, which we attain by using the reasoning faculties of the mind, and the kind of understanding that can only come from faith.

FAITH TRANSCENDS HUMAN UNDERSTANDING

Kierkegaard celebrates "infinite resignation" as the penultimate station on the journey to faith. If you look at how the story of the binding of Isaac turns out, says Kierkegaard, you might be moved to believe. But that hardly exhausts the significance of this drama. We must try to imagine for ourselves the way it must have felt to Abraham, before he knew its final outcome. His willingness to sacrifice the son for whom he had waited for so many years exceeds what can possibly make sense to the powers of reason. His willingness can only, says Kierkegaard, inspire amazement. Abraham's absolute faith is the issue here. Anything else robs the story of its full dimension, flattens it out, trivializes it.

> For the movements of faith must constantly be made by virtue of the absurd, yet in such a way, be it observed, that one does not lose the finite but gains it every inch. (Kierkegaard, p. 48)

Kierkegaard here introduces us to the notion that faith is absurd—that it does not make rational sense. We do not arrive at faith by using our intellect, but only through a knowledge that has another basis. And yet, as he will elaborate later, when we give something up under the promptings of faith, the paradox is that rather than losing it, we gain it back. Put differently, we cannot possess a thing unless we are prepared to let it go. This idea will be spelled out more clearly very soon.

> Yet Abraham believed and did not doubt, he believed the preposterous. If Abraham had doubted—then he would have done something else, something glorious.... He would have plunged the knife into his own breast. He would have been admired in the world, and his name would not have been forgotten; but it is one thing to be admired, and another to be the guiding star which saves the anguished.
>
> But Abraham believed. He did not pray for himself with the hope of moving the Lord—it was only when the ... punishment was decreed upon Sodom and Gomorrha that Abraham came forward with his prayers.... he did not doubt ... he did not challenge heaven with his prayers. He knew that it was God the Almighty who was trying him ... he knew also that no sacrifice was too hard when God required it. (Kierkegaard, pp. 35–36)

Kierkegaard reminds us that the kind of faith exemplified by Abraham is "preposterous"—it transcends our conventional rational categories. Had Abraham been functioning within those categories, he would have killed himself rather than fulfill the demand that God made upon him. Had he been attached to his own happiness, he might have prayed to God to spare his son, just as he had earlier remonstrated with God on behalf of any righteous people who might be living in the cities of Sodom and Gomorrha, which were to be destroyed as punishment for their wickedness (Gen. 18:23–33). But Abraham does not argue or pray on his own behalf because he has totally submitted himself to the will of God. "If God asks it," says Kierkegaard's Abraham, "then—at whatever cost to my self or my self-interest—it must be done." Isaac was the son of Abraham's old age, the only child that his wife Sarah gave birth to—at the miraculous age of ninety. Yet Abraham does not question God's command. This is what it is to have absolute faith.

> There were countless generations which knew by rote, word for word, the story of Abraham.... What they leave out of Abraham's history is dread [angst] ... to the son the father has the highest and most sacred obligation.... If faith does not make it a holy act to be willing to murder one's son, then let the same condemnation be pronounced upon Abraham as upon every other man.... The ethical expression for what Abraham did is, that he would murder Isaac; the religious expression is, that he would sacrifice Isaac ... it is only by faith one attains likeness to Abraham, not by murder.... If he does not love like Abraham, then every thought of offering Isaac would be not a trial but a base temptation ... I do not however mean in any sense to say that faith is something

lowly, but on the contrary that it is the highest thing. (Kierkegaard, pp. 39–44)

It is faith that transforms Abraham's actions from the most heinous conceivable to something worthy, even admirable. On the level of the ethical—that is, the rational—the act warrants our condemnation. It is only as Abraham moves from the realm of the ethical to the realm of faith that the act becomes sanctified. What precipitates that movement from the lower sphere to the higher is angst—the dread that grows from the awareness that there is more to our lives than we can ever know while we remain enmeshed in this temporal, finite realm.

LIVING BY FAITH RATHER THAN REASON

I ... know what ... I would have done. The very instant I mounted the horse I would have said to myself, "Now all is lost. God requires Isaac, I sacrifice him, and with him my joy—yet God is love and continues to be that for me; for in the temporal world God and I cannot talk together, we have no language in common" ... my prodigious resignation was the surrogate for faith.... That I was resolute in making the movement might prove my courage, humanly speaking, that I loved him with all my soul is the presumption apart from which the whole thing becomes a crime, but yet I did not love like Abraham. (Kierkegaard, pp. 45–46)

In the realm of the ethical (that is, the rational—what Kierkegaard sometimes refers to as "humanly speaking") the most we can aspire to is "infinite resignation," the willingness to give up (to sacrifice) what we hold most dear. Kierkegaard calls someone who is willing to give up anything and everything in the name of some abstraction, some greater good, a "knight of infinite resignation." "Humanly speaking," this might be considered praiseworthy. But to Kierkegaard, there is an even more desirable estate that can be aspired to, that of the "knight of faith." As he notes later in *Fear and Trembling:*

> Infinite resignation is the last stage prior to faith, so that one who has not made this movement has not faith; for only in the infinite resignation do I become clear to myself with respect to my eternal validity, and only then can there be any question of grasping existence by virtue of faith. (Kierkegaard, p. 57)

The role of "knight of infinite resignation" is only a way station on the road to a still higher position, "the knight of faith." As we can anticipate, Abraham is the quintessential "knight of faith."

> But what did Abraham do?... he believed that God would not require Isaac of him, whereas he was willing nevertheless to sacrifice him if it was required. He believed by virtue of the absurd.... He believed ... that God would not require Isaac ... but by a double-

movement he had reached his first position, and therefore he received Isaac more gladly than the first time.... He believed by virtue of the absurd.... The last stage he loses sight of is infinite resignation. He really goes further and reaches faith ... the movements of faith must constantly be made by virtue of the absurd, yet in such a way, be it observed, that one does not lose the finite but gains it every inch. (Kierkegaard, pp. 46–48)

Unlike the actions of the knight of infinite resignation—those that Johannes de Silentio imagines himself capable of—Abraham moves beyond the act of surrender. Because of his faith, he is confident that even as he offers Isaac up, he will get him back. What rational explanation is there for such a belief? There is none. His belief exceeds the bounds of reason. It is, to use Kierkegaard's word, "absurd." It makes no sense; his conviction is rooted entirely in faith. But faith is how we connect ourselves to the other side of the great divide. Like all things pertaining to that other side, it cannot be expressed in language or reduced to categories and propositions that make sense to our finite minds. Yet in faith, Abraham is confident that he will not only not lose Isaac, but that he will also gain him. As Kierkegaard asserts, "Only he who draws the knife gets Isaac" (Kierkegaard, p. 38).

> Yet in faith, Abraham is confident that he will not only not lose Isaac, but that he will also gain him. As Kierkegaard asserts, "Only he who draws the knife gets Isaac."

As Kierkegaard seeks to describe the "movement" of the knight of faith, poignant autobiographical elements creep into his account.

> A young swain falls in love with a princess, and the whole content of his life consists of this love, and yet the situation is such that it is impossible for it to be realized, impossible for it to be translated from ideality to reality.... Now we let the knight of faith appear. He makes exactly the same movements as the other knight, infinitely renounces claim to the love which is the content of his life, he is reconciled in pain; but then occurs the prodigy, he makes still another movement more wonderful than all, for he says, "I believe nevertheless that I shall get her, in virtue, that is, of the absurd, in virtue of the fact that with God all things are possible." ... At the moment when the knight made the act of resignation, he was convinced, humanly speaking, of the impossibility. This was the result reached by understanding.... On the other hand, in the infinite sense, it was possible.... This is quite clear to the knight of faith, so the only thing that can save him is the absurd, and this he grasps by faith. So he recognizes the impossibility, and that very instant he believes the absurd. (Kierkegaard, pp. 52, 57)

Of course we cannot help but hear echoes of Kierkegaard's own broken engagement to Regine in this parable. Whether Kierkegaard based his actions on these convictions or chose afterward to interpret his own (erratic) behavior through the prism of this construct is beyond our competence to decide and certainly beyond the scope of this brief chapter. Still, this parable does serve to clarify the contrast between the "knight of infinite resignation" and the "knight of faith," between the realm of the ethical and the realm of the infinite, between reason and faith. The knight of infinite resignation is prepared to give up all that he holds most dear. But the knight of faith lives with the confidence that what he gives up will be restored to him. He believes this despite the fact that it is contrary to reason. It is a conviction that can only be gained by faith, which allows us to transcend reason.

> For the act of resignation faith is not required, for what I gain by resignation is my eternal consciousness, and this is a purely philosophical movement.... The movements are frequently confounded.... In resignation I make renunciation of everything, this movement I make by myself ... and what I gain is myself in my eternal consciousness, in blissful agreement with my love for the Eternal Being. By faith I make renunciation of nothing, on the contrary, by faith I acquire everything ... A purely human courage is required to renounce the whole of the temporal to gain the eternal ... But a paradoxical and humble courage is required to grasp the whole of the temporal by virtue of the absurd, and this is the courage of faith. By faith Abraham did not renounce his claim upon Isaac, but by faith he got Isaac. (Kierkegaard, p. 59)

SUSPENDING THE ETHICAL

Kierkegaard explores yet another dimension of the nature of human faith (a troubling one) under the daunting-sounding rubric, "Is there such a thing as the teleological suspension of the ethical?" The word *teleological* is a philosophical term meaning "the highest end." To rephrase Kierkegaard's question, are any goals so lofty that they trump our ethical obligations? Kierkegaard answers in the affirmative.

> The ethical as such is universal ... it has nothing ... [outside of] itself which is its *telos* [goal or object], but is itself *telos* for everything outside it ... for faith is this paradox, that the particular is higher than the universal. If this not be faith, then Abraham is lost.... Faith is precisely this paradox, that the individual as the particular is higher than the universal ... the story of Abraham contains such a teleological suspension of the ethical. He acts by virtue of the absurd. Abraham's relation to Isaac, ethically speaking, is quite simply expressed by saying that a father shall love his son more than himself.... By his act he overstepped the ethical entirely and possessed a higher *telos* outside of it, in relation to which he suspended the former. (Kierkegaard, pp. 64–69)

Kierkegaard argues that the story of Abraham presents just such an example. Though normal, rational, and even ethical values would prohibit the slaughtering of your own child, such an act, were it to emanate from the sphere of the

Divine, would be required by faith. Thus faith, according to Kierkegaard, takes precedence over normal considerations—even those considerations imposed upon us by our own reason and ethical values. "The absolute duty may cause one to do what ethics would forbid," he starkly declares (Kierkegaard, p. 84). Abraham's actions would horrify us under normal circumstances. His behavior is contrary to what reason would dictate; it violates the ethical standards by which we live our lives and by which he could have been expected to live his. Yet he was faithful to a higher purpose; he acted as he did by virtue of his participation in a realm that transcended the finite realm of ethics and reason. His action embodies the lesson that there is more to human life than is apparent to our senses and even our minds. Abraham felt the pull of the Divine.

> In the story of Abraham we find ... a paradox. ... This ethical relation is reduced to a relative position in contrast to the absolute relation to God. (Kierkegaard, p. 81)

Kierkegaard devalues ethicism by relativizing its obligations. "He who denies himself and sacrifices himself for duty gives up the finite in order to grasp the infinite," he writes (Kierkegaard, p. 71). But who is to determine what is "absolute" and what is contingent, what is divine, and what is worldly? When does our higher duty call upon us to suspend our morality? Kierkegaard's Abraham is not interchangeable with the Abraham of the Jewish or the Christian tradition; Kierkegaard finds dimensions in his story that no one had evoked before him. The Bible and the religious traditions that flowed from it do not employ the phrase "the teleological suspension of the ethical." But it is in Kierkegaard's presentation of this aspect of this issue—stark, startling, and profoundly disturbing—that the distinction between the realm of the ethical and the realm of faith is most sharply drawn.

BUBER AND HESCHEL CRITIQUE KIERKEGAARD

It is noteworthy that neither Buber nor Heschel agreed with Kierkegaard's idea of the teleological suspension of the ethical. Heschel asserts:

> There are few thoughts as deeply ingrained in the mind of biblical man as the thought of God's justice and righteousness. It is not an inference, but an *a priori* of biblical faith, self-evident; not an added attribute to His essence, but given with the very thought of God. It is inherent in His essence and identified with His ways. (*The Prophets,* pp. 199–200)

Buber, for his part, denies that "that which is otherwise purely evil" can ever "become pleasing to God." Abraham, God's chosen one, is a special case. For the rest of us, ethics always prevail.

> God Himself demands of … every man (not of Abraham, His chosen one, but of you and me) nothing more than justice and love, and that he "walk

humbly" with Him, with God (Micah 6:8)—in other words, not much more than the fundamental ethical. (*The Eclipse of God,* p. 118)

Buber and Kierkegaard both agree that the most important dimension of religion—and of human life—is to live in relation to God. Where they disagree is about the validity of the idea that this relationship can ever demand or involve the suspension or transcendence of conventional ethical norms.

It may well be that both Buber and Heschel respond to this idea so strongly because they wrote as Jews in the wake of the Holocaust. Indeed, Buber virtually asserts as much when he says:

Ours is an age in which the suspension of the ethical fills the world in a caricaturized form.... False absolutes rule over the soul, which is no longer able to put them to flight through the image of the true. (*The Eclipse of God,* p. 119)

The suggestion that anything—even religion—could claim to supersede the laws of human morality was not one that either of these refugees from Hitler's Europe was prepared to entertain.

KIERKEGAARD AND THE PHILOSOPHY OF NONRATIONALITY

Unlike many interpreters of religion, both classic and more recent, who insist that faith is in absolute harmony with the categories of rationality and can be explained in the vocabulary of human reason, Kierkegaard insists that faith can only be understood in opposition to the categories of rationality, and certainly in opposition to the conventional patterns of life. For Kierkegaard, faith exists on a wholly other plane. To truly be a person of faith may involve cutting yourself off from the modes and patterns of conventional thought and life. In the case of Abraham, his faith compelled him to violate one of the fundamental "universal principles" of ethical behavior.

In differentiating the realm of faith from that of ethics, Kierkegaard also sets the individual above the universal. Rather than finding the highest good in universal principles, he maintains that it is the individual who, finally, becomes the measure of all things. This emphasis on the individual and individual experiences, rather than on fundamental essences or overarching principles, is a hallmark of the existentialist mode of thought.

Kierkegaard's Abraham acts on his individual perceptions rather than on the universal principles that dominate in the sphere of ethics (as they dominated in the realm of philosophy in Kierkegaard's day). Faith, as Kierkegaard would have us understand it, is not subject to the strictures of "common sense" or even the deepest probings of the intellect. But if faith is ineffable, it is undoubtedly transcendent—it participates in the very infinitude to which its existence attests. As such we cannot expect to make sense of it or of the demands it might impose upon us. The contents or objects of faith cannot, in the end, be explained or defined. Faith and that to which faith attests will always elude the finite and limited categories of the human mind.

A NEW FOCUS FOR
RELIGIOUS DISCOURSE

Kierkegaard did not presume to talk about the object of faith. He did not seek to define or explain God, nor did he offer, as many classical theologians did, proof for the existence of God. He knew this was not possible. What he did speak about were the finite realities that are accessible to all of us. He spoke about the subjective human experience, even the subjective human experience of religion. This change of focus has far greater implications than we might at first appreciate. For with this reframing of the questions to be asked, Kierkegaard radically transformed how the task of the religious thinker was to be conceived. He refocused the subject of religious conversation from the metaphysical, from the infinite that cannot be subjected to the categories of human thought and discussion, to the human experience of metaphysical realities, which *can* be described and, perhaps, understood.

In his remarkable examination of the story of Abraham's binding of Isaac, Kierkegaard gave us the opportunity to examine the meaning of the human quality of faith from an entirely new perspective. Because of his remarkable literary skill, he evoked the experience of being a person of faith.

MARTIN BUBER

The Human-Divine
Conversation:
Religion as Relationship

Martin Buber (1878–1965) is widely regarded as the outstanding Jewish thinker of the twentieth century. A multifaceted, creative thinker, Buber made significant contributions
to a number of different areas of Jewish and general thought,
any one of which would have been sufficient to establish a
great reputation. The first international recognition of his
work came with the embrace by Christian thinkers of his
writing about the "I-Thou" philosophy of relation, though,
as we have already noted, Buber himself regarded that work
as an extension of his earlier, more specifically Jewish studies.
I and Thou and his subsequent works written to elaborate
upon this teaching established Buber as one of the preeminent
thinkers of the twentieth century.

Buber's thought influenced writers in such diverse
fields as philosophy, theology, psychology, and education.
He left a powerful imprint on the public consciousness and
created a phrase and an approach to living that has become
a widely recognized byword. For his "I and Thou" thought

alone, Buber deserves his towering reputation. It is worthy of note, however, that by the time he had published his works in that area, he had already achieved widespread recognition in Jewish circles for contributions of a very different sort.

BUBER AND THE HASIDIC TRADITION

Buber first attained intellectual prominence through his publication of stories from the Hasidic community. Hasidism was a movement founded in eastern Europe at the beginning of the eighteenth century by a charismatic teacher known as the Baal Shem Tov—"Master of the Good Name." Hasidism emphasized the role of the individual's own experience and offered a more immediate, personal means of engaging God. Because of its appeal to direct experience as opposed to learning, it attracted masses of followers among the poor, largely unlearned Jews of eastern Europe. Within a century and a half it had become the dominant expression of Jewish life in eastern Europe. The more worldly, educated, and to a large extent assimilated Jews of western Europe followed a very different path in their religious life and tended to look down on their eastern European brethren and the Hasidic forms that characterized their worship.

From the vantage of today we might not appreciate the magnitude of Buber's introduction of Hasidic material into learned discourse, largely because Buber—and after him more systematic students of this dimension of Jewish life— succeeded so well. But at the time Buber wrote, Hasidism and all of the Jewish mystical tradition enjoyed a particularly low repute. Mainstream Jewish scholars vied with one another in their zeal to heap derision on anything having to do with the mystical strand of Jewish life and thought. As an example, Heinrich Graetz, a distinguished and authoritative historian who wrote a well-regarded history of Judaism near the end of the nineteenth century, titled his chapter on Jewish mysticism "The Jewish Dark Ages." In it, he marshaled such sentiments as:

> The mysticism of [the mystical innovator] Lurya ... degenerated into Kabbalistic trifling ... from its mystical setting received a touch of constraint and unpleasantness, like the laughter of a madman ... full of obscure and meaningless formulas.... These corrupting mystic doctrines did not remain a dead letter, but were forthwith put into practice by their adherents ... came to resemble the light of the will-o'-the-wisps that make the waters of a stagnant marsh gleam with a flickering light. The religious stagnation at the time was glaring indeed; there was a complete heathenism; and what was worse, there sounded no warning voice which recognized the mischief or stigmatized, though ever so feebly, the corruption as it really was. (Graetz, *History of the Jews*, vol. 4, pp. 626–27)

Coming from an assimilated German Jewish background, and being very much an intellectual, it must have taken real courage for Buber to devote years of his life to the study of material that his peers dismissed as trash. It is a tribute to Buber's genius that he worked that denigrated "trash" and presented it to the world as a finely polished, beautifully crafted jewel.

There are scholars who argue that *Tales of the Hasidism: The Early Masters,* the publication of which was Buber's first offering from his years of researching Hasidic material, does not authentically represent the primary sources it is ostensibly based on. It is said that Buber, in reworking the Hasidics' writings, refashioned them into a vehicle for his own mystical and romantic ideas. But that criticism misses the point. Just as Herman Hesse's *Siddartha* is not so much Buddhism as Hesse's Buddhism, Buber's version of Hasidism succeeded in drawing something compelling and significant out of a still-vital strain of Jewish tradition that had long been ignored by the wider Jewish community and was entirely unknown to the world at large. As author Ludwig Lewisohn has put it, Buber's Hasidic studies "will remain a permanent possession of mankind in the form he has given them by virtue of that form which has itself become a part of their message and meaning" (cited in Maurice Friedman's introduction to Buber, *Hasidism and Modern Man,* p. 12). It is perhaps appropriate that Herman Hesse nominated Buber for the Nobel Prize for literature in 1949. In his letter of nomination, Hesse wrote, "He has enriched world literature with a genuine treasure as has no other living author—*The Tales of the Hasidim"* (Friedman, p. 12). Buber would go on to publish essays about the meaning of the teachings of Hasidism in which he sought to relate them to the general human condition. *I and Thou* and his other widely read masterpieces owed their very existence to his early labors in the vineyards of Hasidism.

BUBER ΛS A STUDENT OF THE BIBLE

Buber did much more than write about Hasidism in a specifically Jewish context and the I-Thou relationship in general. He also produced groundbreaking studies of the Bible. With his friend and collaborator Franz Rosenzweig (1886–1929), Buber undertook a translation of the Bible into German that charted a new course. Their translation sought:

> to mimic the particular rhetoric of the Hebrew whenever possible, preserving such devices as repetition, allusion, alliteration and wordplay. It is intended to echo the Hebrew, and to lead the reader back to the sound structure and form of the original. (Fox, p. ix)

Buber and Rosenzweig hoped to fashion a Bible for the ear, allowing it to be "heard" in translation in the same way that it was "heard" in its original Hebrew. As Buber would write, his translation aspired to permit German readers to encounter:

> the Bible as though it were something entirely unfamiliar, as though it had not been set before you ready-made.... Face the book with a new attitude as something new.... Let whatever may happen occur between yourself and it. You do not know which of its sayings and images will overwhelm and mold you.... But hold yourself open. Do not believe anything a priori; do not disbelieve anything a priori. Read

aloud the words written in the book in front of you;
hear the word you utter and let it reach you. (1926
speech, cited in Fox, p. ix)

The statement deserves our close attention. It reflects
Buber's own aural approach to the Bible as well as the
methodology he would adopt in interpreting it in the numer-
ous essays and books he devoted to the subject. Read closely,
it also reflects the I-Thou orientation he brought to all
things. As both translator and interpreter, Buber encouraged
us to enter into an I-Thou relationship with the text. Not just
a polymath, Buber sought to weave the various strands of his
interests into an integrated whole.

But even this does not exhaust Buber's wide-ranging
interests and contributions. He wrote about Jewish-Christian
relations and the philosophy of religion. He had a profound
interest in Zionism and wrote extensively about issues relating to the establishment of a Jewish state. Several of his
works are about purely political subjects. And he was not
only caught up in theory; he also engaged in political activity. While still in Germany after World War I, he, like Paul
Tillich, was active in the religious socialist movement. From
his early years, Buber was deeply engaged in the workings
of the worldwide Zionist organization, and when he moved
to Palestine in the 1930s, he energetically advocated for a binational Arab-Jewish state. Prior to his emigration, while
still in Germany, he edited journals and helped create the
Judisches Lehrhaus, a program of adult Jewish studies in
Frankfurt.

THE HASIDIC ABRAHAM:
RELIGIOUS SPONTANEITY

Needless to say, Abraham was a figure of particular interest to Buber; he appears throughout his work. The following quotation is drawn from one of his Hasidic studies:

> Question: Why is the sacrifice of Isaac considered so glorious? At that time, our Father Abraham had already reached a high rung of holiness, and so it was no wonder that he immediately did as God asked him!
> Answer: When man is tried, all the rungs and all holiness are taken from him. Stripped of everything he has attained, he stands face to face with God who is putting him to the test. (*Ten Rungs*, p. 72)

Here Buber addresses a specifically religious issue in overtly religious terms. For Buber the fundamental question is the encounter with God. But Buber would not have us approach God in familiar, "tried and true" ways, even those of our own established patterns. Rather, he would have such a meeting be fresh, spontaneous, and new. These qualities of newness and spontaneity play a large role in Buber's refashioning of the Hasidic material and in the later exposition of his I-Thou philosophy.

In this commentary on the story of the binding (or sacrifice) of Isaac, Abraham is stripped of all the holiness he has already attained. How much more so, implies Buber, must such a trial demand of us, who have not achieved a fraction of Abraham's merit. The religious experience, asserts Buber, involves standing directly "face to face with God," freed of any constraints, considerations, or factors outside of that immediate encounter itself.

In Genesis 18:8 Abraham was visited by three angels who would announce the birth of Isaac. Abraham provided the angels with hospitality, bringing them cakes and curd and milk and a freshly killed calf.

> The biblical passage which says of Abraham and the three visiting angels: "And he stood over them under the tree and they did eat" [Gen. 18:8] is interpreted by Rabbi Zusya to the effect that man stands above the angels, because he knows something unknown to them, intention. Through Abraham the angels, who were unaccustomed to eating, participated in the intention by which he used to dedicate it to God. Any natural act, if hallowed, leads to God, and nature needs man for what no angel can perform on it, namely its hallowing. (*The Way of Man*, p. 20)

In this selection Buber is drawing upon an authentic tradition of biblical commentary in the Hasidic community. Zusya's interpretation is based on the concept of *kavanah*, the deliberate, conscious intention that we bring to prayer and *mitzvot* (obedience to God's commandments). Through our intentionality we can, according to the Jewish mystical tradition, free the sparks of holiness entrapped in the external shells that are the stuff of this material world. As Buber universalizes this teaching, it becomes a lesson in taking the deeds of our life seriously. Buber's lesson, rooted in the Hasidic interpretation but extending beyond it, directs our attention to the issue of our motivation and attitude as we approach the actions, both those that are clearly consequential and those that are apparently trivial, that make up our lives.

THE HASIDIC ABRAHAM: COMING TO GOD ON OUR OWN

Question: Rashi expounds the words of God: "I appeared unto Abraham, unto Isaac, and unto Jacob" [Exod. 6:2] as meaning "I appeared to the fathers." In what way can this be considered an explanation?

Answer: He who had a father who was righteous and devout is not apt to make a great effort to perfect himself, for he leans on the merits of his father. This is even more true of one whose father and grandfather were both holy men; the mere fact that he is their grandson seems to him like solid ground beneath his feet. But this was not so in the days of the patriarchs: Isaac did not concern himself with the merit his father had acquired, nor Jacob with that of his father and his ancestors, for they did not want to be grandsons, but fathers. (*Ten Rungs,* p. 50)

Buber's discussion of the merits of the fathers and the grandfathers sheds light on his own self-understanding. His biographer Maurice Friedman tells us:

> Because of the divorce of his parents, from the age of
> three until fourteen [Buber] was reared in the home
> of his Galician grandfather. Solomon Buber was at
> once a merchant and wealthy land owner, and an
> editor and interpreter of classic rabbinic texts, one of
> the last great scholars of the *Haskalah* [Jewish
> enlightenment]. From his grandfather young Buber
> received his introduction to the world of the Bible
> and Talmud together with a lasting love of Judaism.
> He has described his grandfather as "an elementary
> Jewish being" who "did not trouble himself about
> Judaism," for knowledge dwelled in him and pos-
> sessed his whole person. (Noveck, p. 184)

Still, as with Kierkegaard, it is not the biographical
details that matter with Buber but how he transformed them
into the stuff of thought. In his explanation of Rashi's commentary, he argues against inherited understandings, calling
all people to strike out on their own quest to find their own
answers; to achieve their own accomplishments, to define
their religious lives in their own terms. That this had direct
resonance in Buber's own life is understandable, but the
teaching resonates beyond the merely autobiographical, serving, as Buber intended it to, as universally applicable to the
religious life. Buber, too, was not a grandson, but the
"father" of a unique mode of religious understanding. In
Buber's own words, again:

> The same interpretation has been given to our say-
> ing, "God of Abraham, God of Isaac, and God of

Jacob," and not "God of Abraham, Isaac, and Jacob," for this indicates that Isaac and Jacob did not merely take over the tradition of Abraham; they themselves searched for God. (*Ten Rungs,* pp. 13–14)

The insight is derived from Hasidic thought. But when Buber calls our attention to it, he underscores a theme that has a significant place in his own thought: the fundamental significance of each individual human being. The religious life is not lived vicariously; it cannot be borrowed from the experiences of others, even our direct ancestors. Like Kierkegaard, who directed intense criticism at the official Danish church, Buber was uninterested in the inherited forms of Jewish life. He was not religiously observant and was notably hostile to the particular demands of *halakhah* (Jewish religious law). He did not engage in religious ritual or defer to the norms of traditional practice. What mattered to Buber was the individual's direct, unmediated encounter with God. Thus, in the same manner of Isaac and Jacob, in Buber's rendition of traditional commentary we are called upon not merely to "take over the tradition" of those who went before us but to embark on our own personal search and enter into our own immediate, spontaneous, and utterly individual relationship with God.

Every person born into this world represents something new, something that never existed before, something original and unique…. Every man's foremost task is the actualization of his unique, unprecedented and never-recurring potentialities.

And not the repetition of something that another,
and be it even the greatest has already achieved.
(*The Way of Man,* p. 16)

Here Buber makes explicit the centrality of human individuality in his approach to understanding the human condition. I think it is fair to suggest that the notions of
self-actualization and self-realization are not indigenous categories of Hasidic thought, but must be recognized as concepts imposed by Buber upon the material he has uncovered
and presented to us.

The vignette, about old, blind Bunam underscores this
theme. Since each of us represents something new, and since
each of us is unprecedented and unique, we are of special significance to the world. The world, says Buber, needs what
we, and only we, can bring to it. The world does not need us
to perform someone else's task—this has been done already.
What the world needs is for us to perform our own allotted
role. Buber presented this thought
even more poignantly in his
recounting of a tale about another
Hasidic master, one whom we
have already encountered, Rabbi
Zusya of Hanipol: "Before his
death, Rabbi Zusya said: In the
coming world, they will not ask
me: 'Why were you not Moses?' They will ask me: 'Why were
you not Zusya?'" (*Tales of the Hasidim,* p. 251).

"Before his death, Rabbi
Zusya said: In the coming
world, they will not ask
me: 'Why were you not
Moses?' They will ask me:
'Why were you not Zusya?'"

The notion that every individual has a special role in the
cosmic design that he or she alone can play, and the corre-

sponding demand that each person must not forsake his or her own role for someone else's, resonates with the Hindu teaching of Dharma/life role and task. In the Bhagavad Gita the god Krishna is depicted as instructing his disciple Arjuna, "Better your own Dharma/duty poorly done than someone else's Dharma/duty done well (Bhagavad Gita 3:35). Buber writes: "Everyone should carefully observe what way his heart draws him to, and then choose this way with all his strength" (*The Way of Man*, p. 15).

Buber's outlook is properly called "existentialist" in that it does not ask questions about the ultimate nature of being or about that which we cannot know from our own experience. Rather, as was the case with Kierkegaard, Buber focuses on individuals and how they live their lives. He is particularly concerned that people live in a spontaneous, "in-the-moment" fashion, the better to fulfill whatever is unique and "never-recurring" in themselves. Though derived from a religious context, Buber's insights make powerful sense to people who are not part of the Hasidic, or even Jewish, tradition, and indeed to people who have no faith at all.

RELATIONSHIP AND ENCOUNTER

As noted earlier, Buber and Franz Rosenzweig developed a radically new way of presenting and experiencing the Bible. It involved bypassing the traditional, accepted sources of understanding, the whole Jewish corpus of interpretation that can be found in the Talmud and other rabbinic writings, and throwing yourself into unmediated, direct encounter with the text. Buber's approach to the Divine is reflected in his engagement with biblical texts. Appropriately, he states of the Bible, "This is the teaching about the relation of the God of Israel and Israel" (*The Prophetic Faith*, p. 1).

> The whole Hegira of Abraham is a "religious" event, but the second stage is so in a special sense. The faith becomes something established by necessitating the separation. The God Who goes forth with these men goes not with the sons of Terah, but with His chosen one, who also chose Him. He separates him from them, and sets him in His presence as He is going with him. The God, Who at the beginning was a guardian deity of a man, will become the deity of a community of men; afterwards deity of a people, and finally deity of the peoples; this God Who at the beginning was the deity of a personal, private biography, will become the deity of history; but this combination, this "correlation" of guidance and devotion, revelation and decision, God's love for man and man's love for God, this unconditional relation between Him and man remains. (*The Prophetic Faith*, p. 36)

As we have come to expect, Buber stresses the individualized quality of Abraham's personality, focusing on the manner in which he is separated from all the mediating realities of family, nationality, and so forth. He is left standing on his own, alone in his encounter with God ("The faith becomes something established by necessitating the *separation*"). Indeed it is this act of separation that constitutes his special bond with God ("He separates him from ... [his kin] and sets him in His presence as He is going with him").

The Abraham of Buber reads in no small degree like the Abraham of Kierkegaard. He sacrifices his own volition to the God who "leads man whither He wills," even in opposition to what might be the desires of the individual person himself ("But whither is He leading him? Not to the place whither the man wished to come"). To follow such a God means being willing to abandon what you already know and love in the name of something transcendent.

And the end product of such a willingness to follow where you are being led, the *telos*, if you will, is presented in terms characteristic of Buber's thought: "this combination, this 'correlation' of guidance and devotion, revelation and decision, God's love for man and man's love for God, this unconditional relation between Him and man remains." Buber's presentation of the person of Abraham here becomes understood as an expression of the highest type of I-Thou relationship. Buber's biblical interpretation and his philosophical exposition merge. The Bible, like Hasidic literature, comes to be seen through the prism of Buber's particular way of understanding the human condition.

I-THOU RELATIONSHIP

Buber's interpretation of Abraham's covenant as an instance (perhaps the ultimate one) of man's I-Thou relationship with God is of a piece with his understanding of the human condition, which puts relationship at the center of the human experience. His writings on the subject are dense and can be difficult to unpack at first glance. But he has summarized his fundamental teaching in a single epigram: "All actual life is encounter" (*I and Thou*, Kaufmann trans., p. 62) or, as it has been translated elsewhere, "All real living is meeting" (Smith trans., p. 11). Buber would erect an entire structure of thought out of this fundamental assertion about the nature of human experience. Although we cannot explore the whole edifice here, the following passages give us the opportunity to look at some of its basic elements.

> To man the world is twofold, in accordance with his twofold attitude.
>
> The attitude of man is twofold in accordance with the twofold nature of the primary words which he speaks.
>
> The primary words are not isolated words, but combined words
>
> The one primary word is the combination I-Thou.
>
> The other primary word is the combination I-It; wherein, without change in the primary word, one of the words He and She can replace It.
>
> Hence the I of man is also twofold.
>
> For the I of the primary word I-Thou is a different I from that of the primary word I-It....
>
> Primary words do not describe something that might exist independently of them, but being spoken they bring about existence. (Smith trans., p. 3)

Buber begins with the reality of human subjectivity. All we can really know are states of experience within ourselves.

The world-as-it-is is unavailable to us. Everything we know is refracted through the way we, as individuals, perceive that outer world, and how we take it into ourselves.

We can relate to people or things in the world outside of ourselves in either of two ways. Buber calls these I-Thou (or, as Kaufmann renders it, "I-You") and I-It. The I-It relationship involves regarding things or people outside of ourselves as objects to be used or employed for our own purposes. I-Thou relationships, on the contrary, involve an encounter in which the whole of our selves becomes engaged with the whole of the self of the other. There are no other considerations involved in such an encounter—no thought of utility or putting something to a purpose.

> The world as experience belongs to the basic word I-It.
> The basic word I-You establishes the world of relation. (Kaufmann trans., p. 56)

All that matters is the simple being-in-the-presence-of. It is this that Buber teaches when he writes:

> The primary word *I-Thou* can be spoken only with the whole being. Concentration and fusion into the whole being can never take place through my agency, nor can it ever take place without me. I become through my relation to the *Thou;* as I become I, I say *Thou.* (Smith trans., p. 11)

This meeting with an other is necessary for us to become our full selves. It is in the relation that we achieve our own full selfhood. As Buber writes elsewhere, "Man becomes an I through a You" (Kaufmann trans., p. 80).

"Whoever says You does not have something for its object," Buber writes. "For wherever there is something there is also another something; every It borders on other Its; It is only by virtue of bordering on others. But where You is said there is no something. You has no borders. Whoever says You does not have something; he has nothing. But he stands in relation" (Kaufmann trans., p. 55). Perhaps such ideas sound paradoxical. But we have encountered fundamental truths expressed as paradox before: in the writings of Søren Kierkegaard. The notion that our own reality is shaped by the relations in which we participate is the foundation of Buber's worldview. To him, it is the definitive feature of human experience.

> The notion that our own reality is shaped by the relations in which we participate is the foundation of Buber's worldview. To him, it is the definitive feature of human experience.

As noted earlier, Buber maintains that he derived his I-Thou understanding from his studies of Hasidic material. And though we can argue about how much he brought to Hasidism and how much he took from it, there is no denying that I-Thou and I-It relationships play a major role in Buber's understanding of it. Here he imputes an I-Thou insight to Hasidism's founder:

> The Baal-Shem Tov teaches that no encounter with a
> being or a thing in the course of our life lacks a hid-

den significance ... all contain a mysterious spiritual substance which depends on us for helping it toward its pure form, its perfection. If we neglect this spiritual substance sent across our path, if we think only in terms of momentary purposes, without developing a genuine relationship to the beings and things in whose life we ought to take part, as they in ours, then we shall ourselves be debarred from true, fulfilled existence ... the highest culture of the soul remains basically arid and barren unless, day by day, waters of life pour forth into the soul from those little encounters to which we give their due. (*The Way of Man*, pp. 38–39)

OUR I-THOU RELATIONSHIP WITH GOD

As we have seen in his interpretation of the Abraham story, Buber does not confine his notion of encounter or meeting or relation to the plane of interhuman experience. We certainly can have I-Thou encounters with other human beings. But we can also have I-Thou relations with elements from the realm of nature. And even more significantly, the I-Thou quality must characterize our relationship with spiritual beings.

Here the relation is wrapped in a cloud but reveals itself, it lacks but creates language. We hear no You and yet feel addressed; we answer—creating, thinking, acting: with our being we speak the basic word, unable to say You with our mouth. (*I and Thou*, Kaufmann trans., p. 57)

Later in the book, Buber expands on this idea:

> The extended lines of relationship meet in the eternal *Thou*.
>
> Every particular *Thou* is a glimpse to the eternal *Thou* ... the inborn *Thou* is realized in each relation and consummated in none. It is consummated only in the direct relation with the *Thou* that by its nature cannot become *It*. (Smith trans., p. 75)

Buber describes the relationship between humans and God in terms of his basic understanding of I-Thou relations:

> To include the whole world in the *Thou,* to give the world its due and its truth, to include nothing beside God but everything in Him—this is full and complete relation. (Smith trans., p. 79)
>
> The most powerful and deepest reality exists where everything enters into the effective action, without reserve the whole man and God the all-embracing—the united *I* and the boundless *Thou.* (Smith trans., p. 89)

Buber's interpretation of the idea of chosenness in *I and Thou* is of a piece with the ideas he presents in his interpretation of the Abraham story:

The You confronts me. But I enter into a direct relationship to it. Thus the relationship is at once being
chosen and choosing. (Kaufmann trans., p. 124)

Indeed we hear echoes of this very understanding in another
of Buber's discussions of Abraham. In commenting on the
story of the binding of Isaac, the very same episode that is at
the heart of Kierkegaard's *Fear and Trembling*, Buber
asserts:

> God sees man, and man sees God…. The reciprocity
> of seeing between God and man is directly revealed
> to us. The mutual relationship of the one making the
> demands, who makes them only in order to bless,
> and of the one making the sacrifice and receiving
> the highest blessing in the moment of greatest
> readiness to sacrifice, here appears as the reciproc-
> ity of seeing. God sees the innermost reality of the
> human soul, the reality He has brought out by test-
> ing the soul; and man sees the Way of God, so that
> he may walk in his footsteps. The man sees, and
> sees also that he is being seen…. And now … we
> are shown the perfection of seeing: as a seeing and
> being seen in one. (*On the Bible,* p. 42)

Buber's interpretation of this episode is certainly very
different from Kierkegaard's. Most striking is the way Buber
rests his understanding of the event on ideas such as reciprocity and mutuality. It is the very intensity of the relationship
itself that dominates his interpretation. In many ways, and in

many settings, Buber highlights the I-Thou nature of the human-Divine encounter; he even applies it to direct revelation.

It is possible to imagine that Paul Tillich is implicitly criticizing Buber's relational theology when he writes, "If ... [revelation] is brought down to the level of a conversation between two beings, it is blasphemous and ridiculous" (*Systematic Theology* vol. 1, p. 127). But the fact is that Buber offers an I-Thou interpretation of the concept of revelation that in no way falls into the trivial mode that Tillich anticipates. Buber writes:

> What is it that is eternal: the primal phenomenon, present in the here and now, of what we call revelation?... The essential act of pure relation ... man receives, and what he receives is not a "content" but a presence. (*I and Thou,* Kaufmann trans., pp. 157–58)

With his I-Thou philosophy, Buber introduced a mode of thinking through which he was able to understand and interpret a wide range of the human experience. And in a rare accomplishment for a serious thinker, Buber lived to see the I-Thou concept become almost a household word—and himself a celebrity.

HOW CAN WE SPEAK ABOUT GOD?

We turn to one last Buber—the theologian. At the beginning of *The Eclipse of God* (pp. 6–9), Buber shares a compelling autobiographical vignette that focuses on the meaning of the word *God.* I urge you to read it in its entirety. It is literarily beautiful and a remarkable example of the theological auto-biography.

Buber relates of a time when he was the guest in the home of a man he characterizes as a "noble old thinker." He shares with his host the galley proofs of one of his books that he was reviewing one final time before it was printed. Buber describes how he read the proofs aloud to the old man at the man's request. At the end of the reading, the noble old thinker asked in amazement how Buber could repeatedly use the word *God*. "How can you expect that your readers will take the word in the sense in which you wish it to be taken?" he asked. "What you mean by the name of God is something beyond all human grasp and comprehension, but in speaking of it you lower it to human conceptualization." The old thinker bemoaned the way the name of God has been invoked to justify all manner of hatred and violence. He said that using the name of God had even come to seem blasphemous to him.

Buber agreed with the old man that the word *God* has become distorted by humans. And yet, despite that, perhaps because of that, Buber said he must continue to make use of the term. After all, generations of people have staked their very being on it. They have given their lives for it, and killed others on behalf of it. "It bears their finger-marks and their blood," he said, challenging the man. "Where might I find a word like it to describe the highest!" Any other word might only reflect some form of abstract philosophical speculation, Buber asserted. It could not capture the sense of presence of the One whom all those generations of human beings have meant. As Buber looks at the way human beings make use of the term, he says they draw childish cartoons and scribble the word *God* underneath. They commit atrocities and say they were performed "in the name of God."

And yet—and it is here that Buber began to move toward his essential theological idea—at some point all the posing and insanity fall away and people find themselves standing directly in the presence of God. When we are in the dark night of the soul, said Buber, we stop shouting, "Him … He," and our souls whisper, "You." He imagined all humanity shouting or whispering that "You" in the same single word and then adding to it the word *God*. At that point, "is it not the real God whom they implore, the one Living God, the God of the children of man?"

Buber writes that though the word *God* has been tragically abused, distorted, and misused, we can still venerate it and find its real meaning even in the most challenging of times. He concludes this vignette:

> It had become very light in the room. It was no longer dawning, it was light. The old man stood up, came over to me, laid his hand on my shoulder and spoke:"Let us be friends."The conversation was completed. For where two or three are truly together, they are together in the name of God. (*The Eclipse of God*, p. 9)

Clearly more is presented here than the recollection of a conversation of two kindred spirits. Buber is employing a narrative, rather than a "propositional" format, for the presentation of an idea central to religious thought: what do we mean when we use the word *God?* The "noble old thinker" expresses amazement that Buber would insist on making use of the word since it has become "lowered" and "misused." Clearly the old thinker is responding to relatively recent events (the essay was composed in 1932, though it could have been written in the wake of World War II, or at any other point in history for that matter). Buber has already said of him, "In the last years, which had been war years, reality had been brought so close to him that he saw everything with new eyes and had to think in a new way." We can well imagine him flinching from such wartime slogans as "for God and country" or "God on our side." But Buber argues for holding on to the word "God" despite the uses to which it has been put. Significantly, this conversation echoes another one that Maurice Friedman writes about in his biography of Buber, which occurred when Buber met Paul Tillich for the first time, at a conference of religious socialists in Germany in the early 1920s:

> [Tillich was] a younger man than Buber, well known in certain circles but not yet the world famous Protestant theologian that he later became ... Tillich reported to the larger conference the conclusion that a word should be found to replace "God" in order to unite in the common cause of socialism those who could use this name and those who could not. After he had given this report, Tillich himself has recounted, a short man with a black beard and fiery black eyes stood up in back and said: *"Aber Gott ist ein Urwort!"* [God is a primordial word!] You cannot do away with

a primordial word like God, said Buber, even for the
sake of attaining unity. "And he was right!" Tillich
exclaimed. (Friedman, Vol. 2, p. 99)

But I suspect that the most salient piece of theological
thinking in this narrative is located not in the difference
between Buber and the older man, but precisely where they
are in agreement. At the very beginning of the conversation
the older man asserts, "What you mean by the name of
God is something beyond all human grasp and comprehension." Buber does not disagree with him. Rather he states,
"Where might I find a word ... to describe the highest! If I
took the purest, most sparkling concept from the inner
treasure-chamber of the philosophers, I could only capture
thereby an unbinding product of thought. I could not capture the presence of Him." Buber and the "noble old
thinker" agree that the word *God* can never capture the full
reality of God. As Buber states elsewhere, "Whether one
speaks of God as He or It, this is never more than allegory.
But when we say You to him, the unbroken truth of the
world has been made word by mortal sense" (*I and Thou*,
Kaufmann trans., pp. 147–48).

WE CANNOT SPEAK OF THE REALITY OF GOD IN FINITE TERMS

Buber, like Kierkegaard, asserts that the fullness of God's
reality is beyond the human capacity to grasp or express. We
cannot know God as God is in God's infinity. Even less can
we express the reality of God in finite terms. The most we

can do is describe what happens to human beings when they are in relation to God. We recognize that whatever terms we use to describe infinity are, at best, dim evocations of what that reality is. For Buber, the best we can do is employ "allegories." Buber makes the clear distinction between the word *God* and the "highest" to which it refers. This idea will be discussed more fully in the thought of Paul Tillich, who prefers to describe the finite words we use to express the infinite as "signs" or "symbols."

Buber distinguishes between the arid "idea" of God and the reality of God. As with Kierkegaard, his concern is not with rational categories, but with lived experiences. He speaks of God in relational terms, asserting that rather than saying "He, He" we should sigh or shout "Thou." It is only in the lived experience of relationship that we begin to intimate God in all of God's transcendent reality.

Indeed, given the lens through which Buber examined the human condition, it is fair to suggest that perhaps the most significant thing about the vignette of the "noble old thinker" is not the position that either man took about the validity of the continued use of the word *God*, or even their agreement that the word does not begin to contain the ultimate reality that it denotes. Rather, I suspect that what Buber wants us to absorb from this account is the very fact of their meeting—a meeting at the most profound level. These two thinkers, each with significantly different perspectives on the most important of issues, encountered one another in the fullness of their being: "It had become very light in the room ... The old man stood up, came over to me, laid his hand on my shoulder and spoke: 'Let us be friends.'" Here is a compelling example of a true I-Thou encounter, conducted, as it were, in the name of God.

Multifaceted thinker that he was, Buber made so many original, profound, and lasting contributions to religious thought. Even more impressively, he managed to find the points of convergence in all of his different areas of interest, weaving his ideas into a whole cloth of insight that has enriched the way we conceive of religious experience. Moreover, it has enlarged the way we understand the most significant dimensions of the human condition.

PAUL TILLICH

The Quest for "The God Above God"

In an autobiographical sketch Paul Tillich (1886–1965) describes his life and work in biblical terms, relating his own personal and spiritual journeys to those of the biblical Abraham:

> The boundary between native land and alien country is not merely an external boundary marked off by nature or by history. It is also the boundary between two inner forces, two possibilities of human existence, whose classic formulation is the command to Abraham: "Go from your home ... to the land that I will show you" (Gen. 12:1). He is bidden to leave his native soil, the community of his family and cult, his people and state for the sake of a promise that he does not understand. The God who demands obedience of him is the God of an alien country, a God not bound to the local soil, as are pagan deities, but the God of history, who means to bless all the races of the

earth. This God, the God of the prophet and of Jesus, utterly demolishes all religious nationalism—the nationalism of the Jews, which he opposes constantly and that of the pagans, which is repudiated in the command to Abraham. For the Christian of any confession, the meaning of this command is indisputable. He must ever leave his own country and enter into a land that will be shown to him. He must trust a promise that is purely transcendent…. The command to go from one's country is more often a call to break with ruling authorities and prevailing social and political patterns, and to resist them passively or actively. It is a demand for "spiritual emigration" … The path into an alien country may also signify something wholly personal and inward; parting from accepted lines of belief and thought; pushing beyond the limits of the obvious; radical questioning that opens up the new and uncharted … It is a temporal, not a geographical emigration. The alien land lies in the future, the country "beyond the present." And when we speak of this alien country we also point to our recognition that even what is nearest and most familiar to us contains an element of strangeness. This is the metaphysical experience of being alone in the world that existentialism takes as its expression of human finitude.

In every sense of the word, I have always stood between native and alien land. I have never decided exclusively for the alien, and I have experienced both types of "emigration." I began to be an "emigrant" personally and spiritually long before I actually left my homeland. (*On the Boundary,* pp. 91–93)

In these brief paragraphs Tillich reveals so much about his personal reality and his thought. Born in Brandenberg, Germany, Tillich, like his father, was ordained as a Lutheran pastor. In 1933 he was fired from his university position because of his outspoken opposition to the Nazis. When Reinhold Niebuhr offered him a job at the Union Theological Seminary in New York, he moved to the United States; he became a citizen in 1940. It is appropriate to begin our discussion of Tillich with his reflections on his own life, for in his thought he argues that we must always begin with the facts of human life before we can move from there to the realm of ideas.

TILLICH'S LIFE AND THOUGHT AS A "JOURNEY"

It makes sense that Tillich titled his biographical sketch *On the Boundary,* for in his life and work he did indeed place himself between many different worlds. While still in Germany, he taught both philosophy and theology. A political activist—like his friend Martin Buber, he was involved in the religious socialist movement—Tillich was always fascinated by the religious implications of the life of the broader culture.

His task, as he defined it for himself, was to harmonize the different realms he inhabited. As a "translator" of religious ideas, his goal was to make religion, and the contents of his particular religious tradition, comprehensible to those who were not of that tradition or who may have even been nonreligious. He sought to create a bridge between faith and the modern world. He strove to help the nonbeliever understand the experience of faith and to aid believers in clarifying dimensions of their own faith by applying the insights of modern culture.

As he intimates in this sketch, Tillich was very much a journeyer. In his thought he traveled, rather fearlessly, from the known into the unknown, into "the new and uncharted." He never hesitated to "push ... beyond the limits of the obvious." The result of his efforts at translation was a provocative and challenging way to understand the meaning of religion and, not unlike what we have seen expressed already by Buber, especially the meaning of that most important and freighted religious word, *God*.

Like Abraham, Tillich was forced to leave his ancestral land and travel to a new and, for him, uncharted world. His self-identification with the biblical patriarch has more metaphorical overtones as well. Like Abraham, Tillich would remain a journeyer all his days, traveling to new places, and more significantly, traveling to new ideas and new ways of understanding. Intellectually, Tillich, in Abraham's footsteps, was very much a bedouin. And like Abraham, his life was marked by a certain restlessness that never allowed him to feel settled.

All of this is intimated in the previous selection from *On the Boundary*. What Tillich does not elaborate is another facet of the biblical verses to which he alludes. The biblical Abraham is called on to leave his "father's house." And here, I suspect, we come to what may have been the most wrenching part of Tillich's journey. His father was a prominent Lutheran pastor; thus Tillich's career began in that familiar intellectual, spiritual, and religious environment. But over time he would find himself wandering from it. I cannot help but wonder whether his omission of this aspect of the story of Abraham reflects the fact that the pain of that part of his journey was still too fresh for him to confront. In any event, his journey did take him far away from the conventional religious understandings he had grown up with and moved him to explore significant new ways of understanding his own, and humanity's, religious situation.

I also cannot help but wonder whether, in using the story of Abraham as the pattern for his own life, Tillich was not suggesting that he, too, was the founder of a whole new way of understanding. Abraham, after all, is called "the first monotheist." Is it possible that Tillich believed that his own work created an entirely new, indeed revolutionary, religious perspective? At the very least Tillich blazed trails that he hoped the rest of us would follow. The biblical Abraham received a promise, "In you shall all the families of the earth be blessed" (Gen. 12:3). Out of Tillich's journey, his lifelong quest to push beyond the boundaries of his patrimony, he gave us all the gift of new perspectives and new horizons. Like all explorers, Tillich bequeathed us a wider world.

THE INFINITE AND THE FINITE

Like Kierkegaard and Buber, Tillich's orientation was existential. Throughout his work he acknowledged the impossibility of discussing that which lies beyond the realm of our senses.

Much of his writing was devoted to arguing that the terms we use for that reality are but symbols for what cannot be expressed in the finite terms of the everyday world. Instead of directing his attention to the unknown, Tillich, as both Kierkegaard and Buber before him, addressed the reality of the human situation on this side of that great divide between the human and the Divine. He wrote about what it is like to be a person of faith who firmly believes in the transcendent, but who can only express his apperceptions of the Divine in the limited terms and symbols we have available to us.

Since we have begun with Tillich's presentation of his own life through a consideration of one episode from the life of Abraham, let us continue our study of Tillich's thought by exploring the way he understands one means of encountering the infinite: the Bible. For Lutherans, the Bible is a direct revelation; its words are God's words. These brief excerpts from Tillich's book *Biblical Religion and the Search for Ultimate Reality* suggest how far from his father's religious orientation he had wandered:

> Religion is a function of the human mind; according to recent theologians, it is the futile attempt of man to reach God. (p. 2)

> Revelation must be received and ... the name of the reception of revelation is "religion."... Revelation is

never revelation in general, however universal its claims may be. It is always revelation for someone and for a group in a definite environment, under unique circumstances. Therefore, he who receives revelation witnesses to it in terms of his individuality and in terms of the social and spiritual conditions in which the revelation is manifested to him ... The Bible is a document both of the divine self-manifestation and of the way in which human beings have received it. (pp. 3–4)

There is no pure revelation. Wherever the divine is manifest it is manifest in ... a concrete physical and historical reality, as in the religious receptivity of the biblical writers. (p. 5)

In Tillich's interpretation of the religion of the Bible, we can recognize the same great divide we saw in Kierkegaard between the infinite world that we cannot know in its own terms and the finite world of which we are part. After all, "reason ... is finite and therefore unable to grasp the infinite" (p. 64). In this presentation Tillich refers to the reality of God as the "ultimate reality beyond everything that seems to be real," "being-itself," or "the power of being in everything that is." This ultimate reality cannot be known in its own terms.

For Tillich, revelation is not the absolute "pure" self-disclosure of the infinite. That would be impossible. We, with our limited capacities, could not receive it. Such divine self-disclosure, as is made available to us, is perceived, recorded, and transmitted in terms of the subjective human reality of those who participate in the experience. "According to every word of the Bible," Tillich writes, "God reveals himself as personal. The encounter with him and the concepts describing this encounter are thoroughly personal" (p. 22). Revelation, as described by Tillich, does not sound all that different from the "essential act of pure relation" of which Buber writes. Tillich himself notes, "Faith is the state of being grasped by the ultimate reality" (p. 66).

For Tillich, the Bible is the product of one such revelation: an act of pure relation as perceived, recorded, and transmitted by one "group in a definite environment, under unique circumstances." We must, Tillich argues, recognize the human component of revelation, the extent to which this document of revelation, as any document of revelation, is a symbol pointing beyond itself to that which cannot be expressed in finite terms.

> When we speak of the "personification" in the religious experience, we attribute all these [personal] characteristics to the bearers of the holy, although they do not actually have them. (p. 24)

We impose a personality on what is essentially impersonal because that is the only way we can grasp it, the only way we can translate the experience into words so as to transmit it to persons beyond ourselves.

> God speaks to man in biblical religion. The *word*, literally taken, is a spoken sound or a written sign, point-

ing to a meaning with which it is conventionally con-
nected. But it is obvious that the God of the Bible
does not speak or hear in this way. His Word is an
event created by the divine Spirit in the human spirit.
It is both driving power and infinite meaning. The
Word of God is God's creative self-manifestation and
not a conversation between two beings ... The Word
is an element of ultimate reality; it is the power of
being, expressing itself in many forms.... But it is not
bound to spoken words. (pp. 78–79)

Tillich, even more systematically than Buber, and certainly more so than Kierkegaard, makes a distinction between
God as God is in God's own terms—what Tillich calls "ultimate reality"—and the way that God is spoken of in terms
that are understandable to finite human beings. For Tillich,
everything that we say about that ultimate reality is a symbol—what Buber calls "an allegory." The symbol, as we shall
see, has value in itself but must not be taken literally in the
way that we would understand the same word or expression
in everyday human usage.

If the transcendent reality of the Divine is inaccessible to
us, we are still driven to seek it and grasp it. "The search for
ultimate reality beyond every-
thing that seems to be real is the
search for being-itself, for the
power of being in everything that
is," Tillich wrote. Tillich speaks

of being "grasped by the ultimate reality." Buber speaks
of much the same thing in *I and Thou* when he describes

revelation as "the essential act of pure relation ... Man receives, and what he receives is not a 'content' but a presence" (Kaufmann trans., pp. 157–58). Revelation, for Tillich, becomes the record of our encounter with that "presence" of the infinite—of God.

THE ULTIMATE REALITY

Man's ultimate concern must be expressed symbolically, because symbolic language alone is able to express the ultimate. (*Dynamics of Faith*, p. 41)

In this single sentence Tillich conveys so much of his religious understanding. As we have already noted, Tillich, like Kierkegaard and Buber, begins with the assumption that there are two worlds, two levels of reality. On one side are all finite things, including human beings, with our limited understanding. On the other side is the infinite.

"Man's ultimate concern must be expressed symbolically, because symbolic language alone is able to express the ultimate."

What is on the other side is incommensurable: our language cannot contain it. Tillich calls this indescribable world the "ultimate reality beyond everything that seems to be real," "being-itself," or "the power of being in everything that is."

Another term he uses has become widely associated with his thought: *ultimate concern*. Unfortunately it has also been widely misunderstood. Some have written that Tillich believes that whatever is most important to you becomes your God. As such, they see the phrase as endorsing a radical relativism, even idolatry. Actually Tillich meant just the opposite. This "ultimate concern" is a way of speaking about what lies beyond. And, says Tillich, it is precisely that which exists beyond our ability to conceptualize or put into words that ought to be most important to us. The highest form of living that human beings can aspire to, Tillich believes, is one that places its greatest priority on its relationship to the ultimate.

But how are we to talk about that which is inherently ineffable? How can man-made words presume to capture the Divine? Tillich's reply is this: the words we use about God cannot be taken literally. When applied to God, those words do not have the same meaning they do when used in terms of things we encounter in everyday human life. We must talk about God/the ultimate, but at the same time we must remain aware that the words we use are only symbols. Buber said much the same thing in his encounter with the "noble old thinker," asserting that anything we say about God is "an allegory." Tillich uses the term *symbol* to make the same point.

SYMBOLS OF THE DIVINE

Tillich differentiates the word *symbol* from a word we tend to use interchangeably with it in everyday speech: *signs*. And it is in his presentation of the differences between these two terms—*signs* and *symbols*—that Tillich moves us deeper into the full implication of his thought:

> Symbols have one characteristic in common with signs; they point to something else.... Signs do not participate in the reality of that to which they point,

> while symbols do…. [Another] characteristic of
> a symbol is that it opens up levels of reality which
> otherwise are closed for us … [a symbol] unlocks
> dimensions and elements of our soul which corre-
> spond to the dimensions and elements of reality … it
> opens up hidden depths of our own being.
> (*Dynamics of Faith*, pp. 42–43)

Tillich is not suggesting that we should not or cannot speak about God, only that we have to keep in mind that our words should not be taken literally.

Tillich does not stop there. He also wants us to have respect for symbols in their own right. The word *exit* painted over a door is a sign that calls our attention to the door beneath it through which we can leave the space we are in. That word *exit* does not take part in the reality of our leaving the room; it merely points to that reality. But a symbol, says Tillich, in some way takes part in the reality of that to which it attests. That is why, for example, some people become so exercised about the treatment of the American flag. For them, the flag participates somehow in the reality of the patriotic spirit it represents. No one would become upset about the defacing of exit signs or stop signs; but the desecration of flags, or of items used in religious services—or of the word *God*—would be very upsetting indeed. In some way symbols participate in the reality they point to. To recast Buber's conversation with the "noble old thinker" into Tillich's terms: even though the word *God* as a symbol of the ultimate reality "beyond all human grasp and comprehension" has been debased and degraded, it still, somehow, participates in that ultimate reality and, for that reason, deserves our respect.

Tillich believes that something about symbols speaks to the deepest part of the human being and evokes awarenesses in us that would otherwise not be aroused. These symbolic words do not mean what they mean in their everyday use; they have the power to communicate to the spiritual parts of ourselves. They communicate to us on a supra-rational level. The appreciation of that part of ourselves that is not merely rational should already be familiar to us from Kierkegaard and Buber.

> Tillich believes that something about symbols speaks to the deepest part of the human being and evokes awarenesses in us that would otherwise not be aroused.

> That which is the true ultimate transcends the realm of the finite infinitely. Therefore no finite reality can express it directly and properly. Religiously speaking, God transcends his own name. This is why the use of his name easily becomes an abuse or a blasphemy. The language of faith is the language of symbols … The fundamental symbol of our ultimate concern is God…. So God is nothing but a symbol?… A symbol for what?… For God! God is a symbol for God. This means that in the notion of God we must distinguish two elements: the element of ultimacy, which is a matter of immediate experience and not symbolic in itself, and the element of concreteness, which is taken from our ordinary

experience and symbolically applied to God.
(*Dynamics of Faith*, pp. 44–46)

The realm of the infinite is so different from ours that it cannot be known to us as it is. We can only talk about it in our own inadequate terms. Of necessity we make use of finite terms to express our experience of the infinite. By a mysterious alchemy, the symbols we use not only denote but also seem to participate in that which they represent.

Here is where Tillich becomes controversial. He suggests that the word *God* itself is merely a symbol. It does not express the fullness of the ultimate. It merely points, directs our attention, toward the ungraspable reality. To imagine that that word in itself captures the whole of God's reality is to be guilty of "blasphemy." That is, we would be confusing the word *God* with the reality of God, which is on the other side of that great divide and can therefore not be expressed in finite terms. Tillich distinguishes between our everyday talk about God, which has to make use of finite terms, and God/the ultimate—as God is in God's reality. Symbols are all we have to express either of them, but we fall into error if we mistake them for the reality of what they represent.

THE COURAGE TO BE

Elsewhere Tillich makes use of another of his provocative catchphrases to describe the idea that the word *God* is (just) a symbol for the reality of God, which is our "ultimate concern" or "being-itself."

The courage to be is an expression of faith and what "faith" means must be understood through the courage to be. We have defined courage as the self-affirmation of being in spite of non-being. The power of this self-affirmation is the power of being which is effective in every act of courage. Faith is the experience of this power. (*The Courage to Be*, p. 172)

With this statement Tillich addresses an issue that is of major concern in his thought: How do we find the courage to exist in the face of the reality of nonexistence? How can we go on living when we know that death is inevitable? These questions reflect the existentialist point of view from which Tillich wrote. In *The Courage to Be*, Tillich answers by stating that we derive our "courage" to exist from our connection with infinite reality. Though we recognize that symbols are all that we have of this reality, by a Kierkegaardian leap of faith, we affirm them:

Every assertion about being-itself is either metaphorical or symbolic ... The divine self-affirmation is the power that makes the self-affirmation of the finite being, the courage to be, possible. Only because being-itself has the character of self-affirmation in spite of non-being is courage possible ... Every act of courage is a manifestation of the ground of being ... By affirming our being we participate in the self-affirmation of being-itself. (pp. 179, 180–81)

Let us take note of the fact that Tillich's term *being-itself* is his way of referring to the ungraspable infinite. We can only talk about this infinite reality by making use of symbols or metaphors (or as Buber would say, "allegories"). It is the reality of that being-itself that is symbolized by our finite word, *God*.

Tillich believes that the object of faith is real. So now we come to the phrase that he employs to express the relationship between our finite word, *God*, and the reality of being-itself:

> The courage to take meaninglessness into itself presupposes a relation to the ground of being which we have called "absolute faith." It is without a *special* content, yet it is not without content. The content of absolute faith is the "God above God." Absolute faith and its consequence, the courage that takes the radical doubt, the doubt about God into itself, transcends the theistic idea of God. (p. 182)

Often when people read about "the God above God" they roll their eyes or shrug their shoulders, stop reading further, and never give Tillich another chance to make sense. Actually the idea is a rather straightforward one that can be explained with relative ease. We have seen it before, in Buber's vignette about his encounter with "the noble old thinker." It forms the basis of Tillich's own discussion of the religion of the Bible.

But first, what does Tillich mean by the phrase "the ground of being"? It is one more symbol, one more label, to describe the indescribable. It is interchangeable with other phrases we find in Tillich's writing, such as "ultimate reality," "that which is of ultimate concern," and "being-itself." It is as if Tillich were being scrupulous not to create one single symbol for something that is so much greater and richer than our vocabulary, lest that one word or symbol come to be confused with the greater reality it points to and becomes the subject of idolatry or blasphemy.

Tillich's purpose in coining the phrase "the God above God" is to underscore the inadequacy of the word *God*. The "theistic idea of God" presumes that God can be understood by science and reason—that there is no ultimate division between the Divine and the worldly, that God and man exist on the same plane. When Tillich derides "theism" he uses the term in a way that echoes Buber's description from *The Eclipse of God* of those who "draw caricatures and write 'God' underneath." The reality of the infinite as it is in itself transcends the symbol we use in our finite language to speak about it. Thus God is above "God." "Theism in all its forms is transcended in the experience we have called absolute faith," Tillich asserts. "It is the power of being-itself that accepts and gives the courage to be" (*The Courage to Be*, p. 185).

The reality of the infinite as it is in itself transcends the symbol we use in our finite language to speak about it. Thus God is above "God."

And yet, by appreciating the significance of symbols for Tillich, we recognize that his referring to the "God above God" does not mean he is utterly dispensing with the word *God* or the symbols that are associated with religious understanding or practice. He recognizes that the word itself and each of those more tangible symbols "participates in the reality to which it points" and must therefore be treated with respect. This brings us full circle to Tillich's discussion of biblical religion, which we examined earlier. Tillich states that "The God above the God of theism is present, although hidden, in every divine-human encounter" (*The Courage to Be*, p. 187). And again, in a different context, "Holy things are not holy in themselves. But they point beyond themselves to the source of all holiness, that which is of ultimate concern" (*Dynamics of Faith*, p. 48).

Symbols are part of our world; nonetheless, they put us into encounter with the world beyond, the ultimate, or the ground of being. Our symbols have profound value for that reason. However, we err if we take our words or descriptions—or stories—literally.

> Literalism deprives God of his ultimacy and, religiously speaking, of his majesty. It draws him down to the level of that which is not ultimate, the finite.... Faith, if it takes its symbols literally, becomes idolatrous! It calls something ultimate which is less than ultimate. Faith, conscious of the symbolic character of its symbols, gives God the honor which is due him. (*Dynamics of Faith*, p. 52)

Among the symbols that have value in this way are the words and ideas of our respective religious traditions, our sacred texts, and the stories they tell. These stories are symbols of the human encounter with the ultimate. And, as symbols, they participate in the reality of those encounters to which they attest. It is in this sense that Tillich understands, and evokes, the story of Abraham that began this chapter.

THE HUMAN EXPERIENCE OF RELIGION

Tillich offers a profound analysis of the forms of the religious experience. He does this by directing our attention, as did Buber and Kierkegaard, to the human side of the divine encounter. Beginning with the same perspective we have already encountered in Buber, Tillich undertakes a more detailed and systematic—we might say disciplined—analysis of the issues. The end product of Tillich's project is very much a unified vision. It begins with the seemingly negative assertion that we cannot know the ultimate reality as it is in its own reality, and that we certainly cannot describe it in finite terms. What we do make use of—and what characterizes the many forms of religious life—are symbols: myths, stories, even language itself. Provocatively, among the words Tillich describes as a symbol is the word *God*. Faith requires no less of a leap for Tillich than it does for Kierkegaard— but, as in Kierkegaard, the object of faith is more "real" than anything that we know through reason or our senses.

Some critics aver that Tillich's vision detracts from the significance of religious life. They ignore the fact that Tillich understood his enterprise to be one of translation. The goal of his intellectual project is to make sense of the religious experience to people who do not speak in the religious idiom. We could add, as well, that he enriches the understanding of the experience of faith for those for whom that idiom is a mother tongue. And we have to acknowledge that, in the goal he set for himself, Tillich succeeded. We cannot grapple seriously with Tillich and be left with a simplistic or superficial understanding of the phenomenon of religion. Like Buber and Kierkegaard before him, he opens vistas on the meaning of what it is to be religious that deepen our own appreciation of that experience and expand our ability to enter into it in the fullness of our selves.

ABRAHAM JOSHUA HESCHEL

God's Need for Man: Faith as a Call to Action

Abraham Joshua Heschel (1907–1972) is widely regarded as the foremost American Jewish thinker of the twentieth century. He established his reputation on the basis of his own scholarship and original thought. But in truth, greatness was a part of his patrimony. Louis Finkelstein, late chancellor of The Jewish Theological Seminary where Heschel taught for most of his years in the United States, and himself an American Jewish luminary, writes of his first meeting with Heschel:

> In the course of conversation we discovered many friends in common, although he derived from one of the most famous Hasidic families in Europe, and Icould trace my ancestry no further back than my great-grandfathers. It was an inspiration to see in my own home a lineal descendant of the famous Maggid of Mezeritch eight generations back and (on his mother's side) from the equally famous

"Compassionate One," Rabbi Levi Yitzchak. He was related by blood-kinship or marriage to almost every important Hasidic "dynasty" in Europe. (Finkelstein, p. 19)

One of Heschel's biographers, Fritz Rothschild, gives us an even fuller account of Heschel's genealogy:

He was the descendant of a long line of outstanding leaders of Hasidism. Among his paternal ancestors he counted Rabbi Dov Ber of Mezeritch, the "Great Maggid," successor to the *Ba'al Shem,* the founder of the Hasidic movement; Rabbi Abraham Joshua Heschel, the Apter *rebbe,* and Rabbi Israel of Rizhyn. On his mother's side he traced his lineage to Rabbi Levi Yitzchak of Berditchev, the famous charismatic Hasidic master, and Rabbi Pinhas of Koretz. (From the introduction to Heschel, *Between God and Man,* p. 7)

Heschel came (both literally and figuratively) from a world in which lineage counted for a great deal. In that world Heschel was royalty indeed. Yet his greatness rests not on the legacy of his ancestors but on what he achieved in his own right.

Heschel was raised as a "prince" and steeped in the learning that defined his culture. And yet, like his biblical namesake Abraham, he chose to leave that world; at the age of twenty he became a student at the University of Berlin. We can imagine the courage and determination it must have taken a young man to impose such cultural dislocation upon himself. And yet he triumphed.

When barbarism descended upon his new world, Heschel emigrated for the second time. As he had from the traditional world of his youth to the post-Enlightenment world of Germany, now he traveled again, first to England and then to the United States, which would be his home for the remainder of his life. Like Paul Tillich, a traveler between places and cultures, Heschel too assumed the role of translator, interpreting the forms and contents from one of his civilizations to the other.

Representative of Heschel's remarkable protean quality and adaptiveness, and his skill as a translator, is the magnificent eloquence of the books he wrote in America. So gracefully does he express himself that it is possible to forget that English was not his mother tongue but a language he acquired later in life. Those in a position to know say he wrote with the same poetic style in German and Hebrew, though neither of those was his native language either.

To most of the American public, Heschel is best known for his engagement in social issues. Reuven Kimelman has written:

Abraham Joshua Heschel lived out his name. As Abraham, he possessed that distinctive combination of compassion and justice. "He kept the way of the Lord by doing what is just and right." He risked his life, his reputation, the affection of his friends and colleagues to fight for the disenfranchised of this world. At the same time, he could pray for and even forgive those who offended him. Some called him Father Abraham.

Heschel marched for civil rights with Martin Luther King Jr. and protested the war in Vietnam. He spoke at the White House Conference on Aging and worked on behalf of the freedom of Jews in the Soviet Union. He became deeply involved in the work of interfaith dialogue and served as a representative of the Jewish community to the Vatican during the deliberations of Vatican II. During his lifetime, many called Heschel a prophet for our time, "speaking truth to power" and serving as a spokesman for the better angels of our conscience. And when he died it was largely in this capacity that he was mourned.

But Heschel was, above all, a scholar and an original thinker. His greatest legacy will undoubtedly be in the writing he has left us. He wrote on a wide range of subjects: the Bible, medieval Jewish philosophy, Hasidism, and popular expositions of such significant Jewish themes as the meaning of the Sabbath, the Jewish community of eastern Europe, and the Land of Israel. He brought to all of these subjects a depth of learning, rigorous scholarship, and precision. He also addressed each of them with the methodology that he would come to call "depth theology," in which he would explore a religious phenomenon from a variety of perspectives in order to uncover the inner meaning that lay beneath its exterior form. This technique reflects significant affinity with someone employed in the general study of religions, which is called the phenomenology of religion.

It is easy to underestimate Heschel. The lyrical and poetic quality of his writing and the very nature of his methodology caused many readers to overlook the profundity of his intellectual enterprise. To some he looked more like a master homiletician than a significant thinker. His technique of holding up a religious phenomenon, turning it around, examining it from multiple perspectives—all for the purpose of eliciting its inner meaning—allowed many to imagine that he was merely being descriptive when in fact he was exploring new perspectives, offering new insights, and, hopefully, eliciting in the reader a sense—an intuition—of its deepest significance.

HESCHEL'S ABRAHAM

The deceptive simplicity of Heschel's work is illustrated by a story he included in a speech he gave on January 31, 1967, during the Vietnam War. Its subject, appropriately for this book, was his first encounter with the story of the binding of Isaac.

A child of seven was reading the chapter that tells of the sacrifice of Isaac [Gen. 22]: Isaac was on the way to Mount Moriah with his father; then he lay on the altar, bound, waiting to be sacrificed. My heart began to beat even faster; it actually sobbed with pity for Isaac. Behold, Abraham now lifted the knife. And now my heart froze within me with fright. Suddenly, the voice of the angel was heard: "Abraham, lay not your hand upon the lad, for now I know that you fear God." And here I broke out in tears and wept aloud. "Why are you crying?" asked the rabbi. "You know that Isaac was not killed." And I said to him, still weeping, "But, rabbi, supposing the angel was a second too

> late?" The rabbi comforted me and calmed me by
> telling me that an angel cannot come late. An angel
> cannot be late, but man, made of flesh and blood,
> may be. (Polner and Goodman, p. 152)

At first reading, Heschel appears to be speaking in the conventional language of traditional Jewish religion, expressing what we would call pre-modern perspectives on familiar religious phenomena. But with Heschel there is always something more at work. And it is that something more that earns Heschel the right to be considered a serious thinker.

Heschel appears to be telling a simple incident from his own childhood. But of course, given the setting of the speech, we can recognize that he has a rhetorical purpose for telling this story—he wants to make a specific point. So we might be moved to dismiss—or acclaim—Heschel as a masterful sermonizer. But the fact is that even in this apparently simple account, many of Heschel's fundamental theological perspectives are on display.

HOW WE LIVE LIFE MATTERS

Heschel begins with a life situation—here his own childhood encounter with the ancient tale—and from there moves on to confront profound issues. Our deepest lessons emerge from life as we live it; life takes precedence over philosophical abstraction. Heschel's emphasis on concrete human experience, not theoretical speculation, is entirely in keeping with his existential orientation. As he has written elsewhere:

The term "God of Abraham, Isaac, and Jacob" is semantically different from a term such as "the God of truth, goodness and beauty." Abraham, Isaac, and Jacob do not signify ideas, principles or abstract values. Nor do they stand for teachers or thinkers, and the term is not to be understood like that of "the God of Kant, Hegel, and Schelling." Abraham, Isaac, and Jacob are not principles to be comprehended but lives to be continued.... (*God in Search of Man*, p. 201)

Initially Heschel invites us to see this well-known story of Abraham and Isaac from the perspective of a seven-year-old, to imagine the anxiety and terror that a young child could be expected to experience from it. But by the time we come to the end of Heschel's account, he is addressing us as adults and eliciting a very different set of concerns, both from the biblical text and from his own life experience.

More telling is another of Heschel's shifts in perspective. In the person of the seven-year-old, he worries about the angel. As the adult retelling this childhood experience, he redirects our attention to the actions of human beings. That is, Heschel begins with a focus on the other side of the great divide. The child's concern with angels is appropriate for an age when human beings think in concrete terms. As we grow older we come to understand that what is on the other side of that divide cannot be known to us in its reality. Angels and other celestial beings are symbols we employ to deal with things pertaining to the "ultimate reality" that is beyond our ability to comprehend or express. But by the end of the account Heschel has redirected our attention to what *can* be known—and he addresses the issue of human conduct. Heschel has performed the maneuver, which we have already experienced in Kierkegaard, Buber, and Tillich, of shifting our attention from what we cannot know to what we can. This is hardly a pre-modern perspective.

THE SUBJECT OF RELIGIOUS THOUGHT IS THE ACT OF BELIEVING

As one close reader of Heschel has written, what Heschel gives us is "descriptive of the ... religious experience ... [but he] defines nothing"—he does not speak of "essences." Indeed Heschel himself, describing another of his projects, notes, "The theme of theology is the content of believing. The theme of the present study is the act of believing" (*God in Search of Man*, p. 7). Heschel studies the phenomena of the human religious experience. In this he continues the path blazed by Kierkegaard and trod as well by Tillich and Buber.

"The theme of theology is the content of believing. The theme of the present study is the act of believing."

Lest we assume that this redirection of our attention is done inadvertently or innocently, let us examine an excerpt from one of Heschel's more systematic discussions of religious issues.

How should the question about the nature of the prophets' understanding of God be asked? The form in which the question is usually put—what is the prophets' idea of God?—is hardly adequate.

Having an idea of friendship is not the same as having a friend or living with a friend, and the story of a friendship cannot be fully told by what one friend thinks of the being and attributes of the other friend. The process of forming an idea is one of generalization, or arriving at a general notion from individual instances, and one of abstraction, or separating a partial aspect or quality from a total situation. Yet such a process implies a split between situation and idea, a disregard for the fullness of what transpires, and the danger of regarding the part as the whole. An idea or theory of God can easily become a substitute for God, impressive to the mind when God as a living reality is absent from the soul.

The prophets had no theory or "idea" of God. What they had was an *understanding*. Their God-understanding was not the result of a theoretical inquiry, of a groping in the midst of alternatives about the being and attributes of God. To the prophets, God was overwhelmingly real and shatteringly present. (*The Prophets,* p. 221)

The philosophical presuppositions that underlie all of Heschel's work are on display here. He distinguishes between the idea of God and the reality of God, a distinction we have encountered previously in Buber and Tillich. As he writes elsewhere:

God cannot be distilled to a well-defined idea. All concepts fade when applied to His essence. To the pious

> man knowledge of God is not a thought within his grasp, but a form of thinking in which he tries to comprehend all reality. (*Man Is Not Alone,* p. 108)

> Genuine prayer is an event in which man surpasses himself. Man hardly comprehends what is coming to pass. Its beginning lies on this side of the word, but the end lies beyond all words. (*Man's Quest for God,* p. 29)

An idea, at best, serves as what Buber calls an allegory and Tillich calls a symbol. Like Tillich, Heschel is concerned that "an idea or a theory of God can easily become a substitute for God"—an error that Tillich would call "idolatry."

WE CANNOT KNOW GOD
WITH OUR MINDS

Heschel treats the idea of God very much as if it were a symbol. Elsewhere Heschel elaborated on the meaning of symbols:

> A distinction ought to be made ... between *real* and *conventional* symbols. A *real symbol* is a visible object that represents something invisible; something present representing something absent. A real symbol represents, *e.g.,* the Divine because it is assumed that the Divine resides in it or that the symbol partakes to some degree of the reality of the Divine. (*Man's Quest for God,* p. 118)

Like Tillich, Heschel is aware of the danger inherent in symbols. When we confuse the symbol for the reality it attests to, the word for that to which the word points, we are guilty of blasphemy. Heschel does not aspire to articulate ideas about the "being and attributes" of God. Instead he explicates the experience of knowing that you are in the presence of God. As with Buber, his subject is the human-Divine encounter.

For Heschel, as for the other members of our quartet of thinkers, philosophical investigation is not an adequate means of knowing God. We cannot grasp with our finite minds the infinite "ground of being," to use Tillich's term. We can only know God, says Heschel, by experience or intuition. As he writes elsewhere, "Long before we attain any knowledge about His essence, we possess an intuition of a divine presence" (*Man Is Not Alone*, p. 67). It is not intellectual inquiry that will allow us to engage God, but a more profound, immediate human sensibility. It is not reason that is paramount in the religious life, but experience.

Heschel frequently made much of the inherent limitations of human knowledge:

> We live on the fringe of reality and hardly know how to reach the core. What is our wisdom? What we take account of cannot be accounted for. We explore the ways of being but do not know what, why or wherefore being is. (*God in Search of Man*, p. 56)

> The world is something we apprehend but cannot comprehend. (p. 57)

> All we have is an awareness of the presence of the mystery, but it is a presence that the mind can never penetrate. (pp. 61–62)

Heschel is emphatic that what is most important cannot be known through reason. As he writes elsewhere:

> To become aware of the ineffable is to part company with words. The essence, the tangent to the curve of human experience, lies beyond the limits of language. The world of things we perceive is but a veil. Its flutter is music, its ornament science, but what it conceals is inscrutable. Its silence remains unbroken; no words can carry it away. (*Man Is Not Alone,* p. 16)

Ursula Niebuhr has quoted Heschel as saying:

> Sensitivity to the mystery of living is the essence of human dignity. It is the soil in which our consciousness has its roots, and out of which a sense of meaning is derived. Man does not live by explanations alone, but by a sense of wonder and mystery. (Niebuhr, "Notes on a Friendship")

WE MEET GOD IN ENCOUNTER

The earlier selection from *The Prophets* makes explicit the fact that for Heschel, as for Buber, encounter, not intellectual understanding, is the goal of religious life. It is significant that at the beginning of his argument against pursuing an idea of God, Heschel uses as his counterargument the example of friendship. The most important thing is not to understand God (which, in the end, will prove impossible) but to be in relationship with God. Heschel has articulated this same significant distinction elsewhere:

There are two types of thinking; one that deals with *concepts* and one that deals with *situations*.... Conceptual thinking is an act of reasoning; situational thinking involves an inner experience ... Conceptual thinking is adequate when we are engaged in an effort to enhance our knowledge about the world. Situational thinking is necessary when we are engaged in an effort to understand issues on which we stake our very existence.... The attitude of the conceptual thinker is one of detachment;... the attitude of the situational thinker is one of concern ... The beginning of situational thinking is not doubt, detachment, but amazement, awe, involvement. (*God in Search of Man*, p. 5)

What Heschel calls conceptual thinking is what Kierkegaard would have called a mode of inquiry that belongs to the realm of the ethical, and what we would characterize as the approach of philosophy. Heschel's situational thinking comes from inner experience, what we, elsewhere, refer to as intuition. This belongs to the realm that Kierkegaard identified as faith. It is noteworthy that Heschel describes its attitudes as being those of "amazement, awe"—qualities we associate with faith—and "involvement." This last quality is one we associate with relationship. In another passage of *The Prophets*, Heschel emphasizes that the goal of religion is not knowledge but action, not ideas in themselves but what they lead to.

The autonomy of ideas may result in their isolation or even in regarding them as independent, eternal, self-subsisting essences. To the prophets, the attributes of God were drives, challenges, commandments, rather than timeless notions detached from His Being. They did not offer an exposition of the nature of God, but rather an exposition into man and His concern for man. They disclosed attitudes *of* God rather than ideas *about* God. (p. 221)

Heschel begins this observation with the standard existentialist critique of philosophy, which rests on "essences."

Heschel is less concerned with what God is than with how human beings respond to God.

Existentialist thought rejects the possibility of "independent, eternal, self-subsisting essences." Even more significantly, Heschel, in directing our aspirations away from the understanding of essences, redirects our attention to "drives, challenges, commandments." Heschel is less concerned with what God is than with how human beings respond to God. Just as he worries less about whether an angel can be late than about whether human beings can be late, he urges us to bypass reflection on the attributes of God and to concentrate instead on the behaviors human beings manifest as a result of their encounters with God.

In Heschel's understanding this distinction is true not only for prophets; it is the goal of every human being. In one of his best-known works, *The Earth Is the Lord's,* which many read as his eulogy for the destroyed world from which he came, Heschel describes the religious life of "The Devout Men of Ashkenaz":

[They exemplified] … the ideals of mystic piety. No high intellectual powers were necessary for the attainment of these ideals: the main requirements being faith, a pure heart, inwardness. Piety was thought to be more important than wisdom; candor ranked higher than speculation; the God-fearing man above the scholar. (p. 65)

Heschel notes that the prophets did differ from ordinary mortals in a significant way:

[The prophets] were endowed with a receptivity to the presence of God. The presence and anxiety of God spoke to them out of the manifestations of history. They had an intuitive grasp of hidden meanings, of an unspoken message. (*The Prophets,* p. 222)

What sets the prophets apart from ordinary people is the heightened nature of their receptivity to God's presence. But it is a difference of degree; potentially all people can experience that presence. Most significantly, Heschel tells us that what the prophets grasped was a hidden meaning. What they heard was an unspoken message. Their revelatory experience derived from their relationship to the Divine rather than any explicitly ideational content. As Heschel wrote, "The act of revelation is a mystery, while the record of revelation is a literary fact, phrased in the language of man." (*God in Search of Man*, p. 258)

The Harvard Law School professor Alan Dershowitz is no expert on Heschel, but he does capture the essence of Heschel's view of revelation when he writes:

> Some contemporary commentators—most notably Abraham Joshua Heschel—argue that the Bible itself is midrash. Heschel regards the central event of biblical theology—the revelation at Sinai—as a midrash about how the law was given to the people of Israel. To take the narrative literally and believe that God actually spoke and handed over tablets is, Heschel argues, to confuse metaphor with fact. According to this view, there is *only* midrash, followed by midrash upon midrash. The stories of the Bible translate God's unknowable actions into familiar human terms that a reader can understand. (Dershowitz, p. 17)

By midrash Dershowitz means "interpretation." This is not all that different from Buber's notion of revelation as "the essential act of pure relation ... Man receives, and what he receives is not a 'content' but a presence" (*I and Thou,* Kaufmann trans., pp. 157–58). When Heschel speaks of the prophets' "intuitive grasp of hidden meanings" we can hear echoes of Tillich's phrase, "grasped by the ultimate reality." What tradition speaks of as revelation is for Heschel, no less than for Buber and Tillich, the result of the direct and powerful encounter of human beings with the infinite. Heschel makes this explicit a few paragraphs later: "To the prophet, knowledge of God was fellowship with Him, not attained by

syllogism, analysis, or induction, but by living together"
(*The Prophets*, p. 223).

> Prophecy consists in the inspired communication of
> divine attitudes to the prophetic consciousness....
> The divine pathos is the ground-tone of all those atti-
> tudes. A central category of the prophetic under-
> standing for God, it [divine pathos] is echoed in
> almost every prophetic statement.
>   To the prophet ... God does not reveal himself
> in abstract absoluteness, but in a personal and inti-
> mate relation to the world. (*The Prophets*, p. 223)

Heschel seems to be employing traditional images of
God, a rhetorical practice that has caused some of his critics
to assume that he was merely dressing up traditional ideas in
modern clothing, however lyrically he might have expressed
them. But Heschel is again operating at a more complex level
than these critics give him credit for. He is not depicting the
ultimate reality in its own terms, but rather is evoking for us
the thought world of the prophets, elaborating on the nature
of what it is that the prophets, here representing all human
beings, intuit about the Absolute. For the prophets, as Heschel
depicts them, God is:

> moved and affected by what happens in the world,
> and reacts accordingly.... He reacts in an intimate
> and subjective manner ... the God of Israel is a God
> Who loves, a God Who is known to, and concerned
> with, man. He ... reacts intimately to the events of

history.... He is personally involved in, even stirred by, the conduct and fate of man. (*The Prophets,* p. 224)

Many have assumed that Heschel is speaking for himself here. Perhaps he is sharing a record of his own intuitions about God's character. It is clear that his intent is not to describe the unknowable reality of God, but the prophet's "grasp of hidden meanings, of an unspoken message." He is writing not about what God is like, but about how the prophets experienced and depicted the God whose presence they had so powerfully experienced and whose nature they had intuited. Heschel writes:

The prophets ... did not simply absorb the content of inspiration, they also claimed to understand its meaning, and sought to bring such meaning into coherence with all other knowledge they possessed.... They experienced the word as a living manifestation of God, and the events in the world as effects of His activity. The given factor, whether the word or the event, was for them an expression of the divine.... Even if the prophets had affirmed the essential unknowability of God, they would still have insisted on the possibility of understanding Him by reflective intuition. (*The Prophets,* pp. 222–23)

Heschel is not writing about the ultimate as it is in its own reality, but about the prophets' intuition of that ultimate and the understanding they derived from that intuition. It is significant and suggestive that he does so by making use of imagery drawn from the most intimate of human relationships: love. In this, he underscores the deeply personal relational nature of the human encounter with God, a relationship he describes as being fraught with mutual pathos, or reciprocally sympathetic feelings.

CAN WE TALK ABOUT GOD'S BEHAVIOR?

Though Heschel adopted the same kind of existentialist orientation we see in the other members of our quartet, he also made use of traditional language to describe God. If he knew, philosophically, that human beings cannot grasp God's attributes, he nonetheless described them. In one television interview he was explicitly dismissive of Tillich's impersonal language:

> One of the most popular definitions of God common in America today was developed by a great Protestant theologian: God is the ground of being. So everybody is ready to accept it. Why not? Ground of being causes me no harm. Let there be a ground of being, doesn't cause me any harm, and I'm ready to accept it. It's meaningless.

Heschel looked for more explicit discussion of God as caring and involved with human beings. Tillich's "ground of being" seemed too abstract and removed from engagement with human beings. Similarly, Heschel was critical of Buber's symbolic understanding of prophetic religion. In *Abraham Joshua Heschel: Prophetic Witness,*

Edward K. Kaplan and Samuel H. Dresner describe a letter Heschel wrote to Buber on June 22, 1935, in which, "while admitting that Buber's emphasis on the prophet's 'symbolic' behavior, directed toward the people, was 'very important and helps clarify many things,' he dwells upon Buber's apparent refusal to consider God's behavior" (Kaplan and Dresner, p. 222). More than any of the other members of our quartet, Heschel evoked a personal God.

IN OUR RELATIONSHIP WITH GOD WE *CAN* REPRESENT GOD

Heschel made frequent use of the term *pathos*. This takes us into one of the most significant dimensions of his thought.

> Never in human history has man been taken as seriously as in prophetic thinking. Man is not only in the image of God; he is a perpetual concern of God. The idea of pathos adds a new dimension to human existence. Whatever man does affects not only his own life, but also the life of God insofar as it is directed to man. The import of man raises him beyond the level of mere creature. He is a consort, a partner, a factor in the life of God. (*The Prophets*, p. 226)

Again and again Heschel underscores the relational nature of the Divine-human encounter. As he writes later in *The Prophets*, "the very ... [name] 'the Holy One of Israel' suggests the relatedness of God" (p. 227). This relational nature is implied in the titles of so many of Heschel's books:

Man Is Not Alone, God in Search of Man, Man's Quest for God. Fritz Rothschild, the editor of an anthology of Heschel's work, captured this idea of relation in the title of his book, *Between God and Man.* Still, even as Heschel asserts the relational nature of the encounter of human beings and the Divine, he understands that the great divide lies between God/the ultimate and our own finite reality. He recognizes that we cannot know the ultimate as it is in itself. What we *can* do is respond to it. What we *can know* is our own response. And it is the nature of that response that is Heschel's primary focus. As he has written:

> How can we ever reach an understanding of Him who is beyond the mystery? How do we go from the intimations of the divine to a sense of the realness of God? Certainty of the realness of God comes about [a]s *a response* of the whole person to the mystery and transcendence of living. (*God in Search of Man,* p. 114)

Elsewhere in *God in Search of Man,* Heschel makes a play on words with Kierkegaard's "leap of faith" when he says that Judaism—and here we can assume he sees Judaism as representative of all religious traditions—calls for Jews to take "a leap of action":

> In our response to His will we perceive His presence in our deeds. His will is revealed in our doing ... A Jew is asked to take a *leap of action* rather than a

leap of thought.... Our way of living must be compatible with our essence as created in the likeness of God ... In our way of living we must remain true not only to our sense of power and beauty but also to our sense of the grandeur and mystery of existence. The true meaning of existence is disclosed in moments of living in the presence of God ... (*God in Search of Man,* pp. 282–83)

What is distinctive about Heschel's thought is that he does not treat the assertion about a relationship as the final statement to be made about God. Rather, it is the starting point for what is unique in his message. Once again Heschel has enacted one of his profound shifts of focus. Though ostensibly writing about God, he shifts the center of our attention to human beings ("a perpetual concern of God"). In his discussion of the "life of God" Heschel will emphasize "the life of man" and stress those things that pertain to "the import of man." As Heschel writes:

The decisive thought in the message of the prophets is not the presence of God to man but rather the presence of man to God. This is why the Bible is God's anthropology rather than man's theology. The prophets speak not so much of man's concern for God as of God's concern for man. (*God in Search of Man,* p. 412)

For Heschel, relationship demands a kind of reciprocity. The human relationship with God demands that we reciprocate

God's concern and caring with our own. Whatever human beings say about God must, in the end, represent something that we can say about ourselves. Heschel distinguishes between this God of pathos and God as described by the German Protestant theologian Rudolph Otto as "the numinous." Otto describes this numinous God as the Wholly Other: fascinating, but radically unlike human beings. Heschel contends that:

> the God of the prophets is not the Wholly Other, a strange, weird, uncanny Being, shrouded in unfathomable darkness.… The numinous is not the supreme category for the prophets.… The primary object of their religious consciousness was a pathos rather than a numen.
>
> Pathos, far from being intrinsically irrational, is a state which the prophet is able to comprehend morally as well as emotionally. (*The Prophets*, p. 227)

Heschel may appear to be contradicting the thinking of the other members of our quartet, but he is actually in concert with them. He concludes this particular reflection by bringing us full circle, back to Abraham and Isaac on Mount Moriah.

> What Abraham and the prophets encountered was not a numen, but the fullness of God's care. The moral law may be obscured, but never suspended. The very act of addressing Abraham was experienced as care. It is because of the experience of God's responding to him in his plea for Sodom (Gen.

18:23ff.) that Abraham did not question the command to sacrifice his only son, and it was the certainty of God's love and mercy that enabled the prophets to accept His anger. (*The Prophets,* p. 227)

We have already taken note of Heschel's strong disagreement with Kierkegaard's concept of the teleological suspension of the ethical. He is most assuredly doing so here. Elsewhere in *The Prophets* he asserts:

God's pathos was not thought of as a sort of fever of the mind which, disregarding the standards of justice, culminates in irrational and irresponsible action. There is justice in all His ways, the Bible insists again and again.

There is no dichotomy of pathos and ethos, of motive … It is because God is the source of justice that His pathos is ethical.

Pathos, then, is not an attitude taken arbitrarily. Its inner law is the moral law. (p. 225)

The very understanding of God conveyed in the term *pathos* makes sense of Abraham's actions in the story of the binding of Isaac. Abraham's knowledge of God's attributes and nature shaped his own being; his understanding of God's actions shaped his own. The issue for Heschel is not what God is, but what our understanding of God makes us become. Our intuition about the "nature and character of God" must be expressed in our

The moral law may be obscured, but never suspended.

actions. Heschel is more explicit about this idea elsewhere. In an essay titled "Man the Symbol of God," he writes:

> There is something in the world that the Bible does regard as a symbol of God.... The symbol of God is *man, every man*.... Human life is holy.... Reverence for God is shown in our reverence for man. The fear you must feel of offending or hurting a human being must be as ultimate as your fear of God. An act of violence is an act of desecration. To be arrogant toward man is to be blasphemous toward God.... The divine symbolism of man is ... in what he *is* potentially. To imitate God, to act as He acts in mercy and in love, is the way of enhancing our likeness. Man becomes what he worships. (*Man's Quest for God*, pp. 124–27)

We may well hear echoes of Tillich's ultimate concern in the statement "Man becomes what he worships." But in a way, Heschel inverts Tillich's concept. He admonishes us that the image we have of God must, in the end, become real through our own attributes. What we perceive as our ultimate concern must become actualized in us.

MAN IS THE SYMBOL OF GOD

Thus we encounter the great paradoxical shift in the focus of Heschel's thought. His theology becomes, in fact, a kind of religious anthropology. In admonishing us that we cannot expect to understand the ultimate, he focuses his attention on what we can know—the finite, human side of the divide. Despite appearances to the contrary, when

"Judaism stands and falls with the idea of the absolute relevance of human deeds."

Heschel writes eloquently and passionately about God, his real subject is man, the symbol of God. Indeed it is this very understanding that is embodied in the title of a poem Heschel wrote when he was still a young man: "The Ineffable Name of God: Man." The more we speak about God's qualities, the more we are saying about human beings' responsibilities. The real nature of the God we worship is attested to by our actions in response to God's presence. As Heschel writes:

> Religion begins with the certainty that something is asked of us, that there are ends which are in need of us. Unlike all other values, moral and religious ends evoke in us a sense of obligation. They present themselves as tasks rather than as objects of perception. Thus, religious living consists in serving ends which are in need of us. (*Man Is Not Alone*, p. 215)

Heschel offers a definition of Jewish religion that also applies, to some extent, to all religious traditions:

> There is only one way to define Jewish religion. It is the *awareness of God's interest in man*, the awareness of a *covenant*, of a responsibility that lies on Him as well as on us. Our task is to concur with His interest,

to carry out His vision of our task. God is in need of man for the attainment of His ends ... Life is a *partnership* of God and man. (*Man Is Not Alone,* p. 241–42)

Judaism stands and falls with the idea of the absolute relevance of human deeds. Even to God we ascribe the deed. *Imitatio Dei* is in deeds. The deed is the source of holiness. (*Man's Quest for God,* p. 109)

In writing about prayer, Heschel expresses an interpretation that reflects his understanding of the entire enterprise of religion:

Prayer is the quintessence of the spiritual life, that is, the climax of aspirations.... to pray what we sense, we must live what we pray.... Our problem is how to live what we pray. (*Man's Quest for God,* p. 94)

In studying Heschel's work we uncover an interesting, perhaps unanticipated, truth. Heschel's renown as a social activist is not something detached and separate from his scholarship. On the contrary, it grows organically from his thought. Our lives, he teaches, testify to the contents of our belief. The attributes of the God to whom we offer prayer are made real through our actions. The ultimate reality that we worship finds expression in our lives.

After marching with Martin Luther King Jr. in a civil rights protest in Selma, Alabama, Heschel wrote that he felt like he was "praying with [his] legs." Many were moved by his turn of phrase. A few critics expressed discomfort that his sentiments sounded too glib. Had they studied Heschel's work, they would have understood that he was speaking literally.

CONCLUSION

Naming the Unnameable: Four Paths to Religious Understanding

Søren Kierkegaard, Martin Buber, Paul Tillich, and Abraham Joshua Heschel—four compelling and fascinating approaches to the meaning of religious life and the religious meaning of human life. Individually and collectively they open windows for us on how to understand our own religious traditions and those of our neighbors. They offer us lenses through which we can explore the question of what it means to be religious.

Four very different thinkers, writing from different religious backgrounds, addressing us in differing idioms in their own singular voices. Each with his own unique angle of vision. And each with his own particular areas of special concern. And yet as we read Kierkegaard, Buber, Tillich, and Heschel in proximity to one another, we cannot help but recognize significant areas of overlapping perspective.

Each of them begins with a recognition of the limits of human understanding. Each expresses humility about the ability of the finite human mind to comprehend the absolute, or to give expression to it. Each recognizes the limitations of reason and embraces ways of knowing the most important things that involve human capacities that transcend the intellectual. Indeed, each identifies those nonrational ways of knowing as the most important way, and perhaps the only way, to perceive the most important realities.

Thus all of the thinkers who make up our quartet devote their intellectual energies not to what *cannot* be known, but to what *can*. They write about realities on this side of the great divide, about the human experience of religiousness, and especially about the human response to our encounter with the ultimate, the ground of being. Each writes about the attitudes and phenomena that characterize the religious life.

Tillich, Buber, and Heschel all share a debt to their predecessor, Kierkegaard. They share, as well, an appreciation of the role of symbols. Explicitly and implicitly all three of these more recent thinkers regard the words and credos of their inherited religious tradition—and those of other traditions—as symbolic expressions of that which cannot be depicted in its own reality. All suggest that the ultimate source of religious inspiration is the God who is above the God that can be spoken of in human language. All three of these thinkers explore language by which we can speak about the infinite. And all suggest that the God worshipped by any person of faith is, in the end, a manifestation of that God above God whose reality cannot be captured by any—or by all—of the symbols that are employed to attest to that ground of being that sustains us.

All four of our quartet of thinkers offer us an image of standing in the presence of a God who transcends all the words that are used to describe or explain the One who is beyond all words and descriptions. They depict faith as involving a personal engagement with the One that transcends all the texts and creeds that constitute our respective traditions. In this, they open a door to the possibility of honoring the traditions from which we come while at the same time recognizing ourselves as standing together in the presence of the One who exists above and beyond all the aspects of the traditions that separate us from one another. Reading them offers us more than knowledge and understanding; it offers us new ways of viewing one another, and of recognizing ourselves as bound together by the profoundest commonality.

Engaging with the ideas of such thinkers may feel perplexing or disconcerting. None of them is particularly easy to read. And they may throw into question our own religious convictions. As any of them would argue, such discomfort is the first step toward developing a congruent and consistent faith commitment. To wrestle with the ideas such thinkers present is to find ourselves challenged to look at our own religious lives in new ways; and to appreciate the spiritual endeavors of others, whatever form their religious expression may take. To engage with these thinkers can leave us enlarged in our perception of human religiousness and deepened in our appreciation of it.

SUGGESTIONS FOR FURTHER READING

Brown, D. Mackenzie. *Ultimate Concern: Paul Tillich in Dialogue.* New York: Harper and Row, 1965.

Buber, Martin, *The Eclipse of God.* New York: Harper and Brothers, 1952.

———. *Hasidism and Modern Man.* New York: Horizon Press, 1958.

———. *I and Thou.* Translated by Walter Kaufmann. New York: Charles Scribner's Sons, 1970.

———. *I and Thou.* Translated by Ronald Gregor Smith. New York: Charles Scribner's Sons, 1958.

———. *On the Bible: Eighteen Studies by Martin Buber.* Edited by Nahum Glatzer New York: Schocken Books, 1982.

———. *The Prophetic Faith.* New York: Harper and Brothers, 1949.

———. *Tales of the Hasidim: Early Masters.* New York: Schocken Books, 1947.

———. *Ten Rungs.* New York: Schocken Books, 1947.

———. *The Way of Man.* New York: The Citadel Press, 1966.

Dershowitz, Alan M. *The Genesis of Justice.* New York: Warner Books, 2001.

Finkelstein, Louis. "Three Meetings with Abraham Joshua Heschel." *Conservative Judaism,* Fall 1973: 19–22.

Fox, Everett. *The Five Books of Moses*. New York: Schocken Books, 1995.

Friedman, Maurice. *Martin Buber's Life and Work*. 3 vols. New York: E.P. Dutton, 1983.

Heschel, Abraham Joshua. *Between God and Man*. Edited by Fritz A. Rothschild. New York: The Free Press, 1959.

———. *The Earth Is the Lord's*. New York: Henry Schuman, 1950.

———. *God in Search of Man*. New York: Meridian Books, 1959.

———. *Man Is Not Alone*. Philadelphia: Jewish Publication Society, 1951.

———. *Man's Quest for God*. New York: Charles Scribner's Sons, 1954.

———. *A Passion for Truth*. New York: Farrar, Straus and Giruox, 1973.

———. *The Prophets*. New York: Harper and Row, 1962.

Kaplan, Edward, and Samuel H. Dresner. *Abraham Joshua Heschel: Prophetic Witness*. New Haven: Yale University Press, 1998.

Kierkegaard, Søren. *Fear and Trembling*. Translated by Walter Lowrie Princeton: Princeton University Press, 1954.

Kimelman, Reuven. "Remembrance of Heschel." *Melton Journal*, No. 15, Winter 1983.

Niebuhr, Ursula. "Notes on a Friendship: Abraham Joshua Heschel and Reinhold Niebuhr." Speech delivered at the College of Saint Benedict, May 16, 1983.

Novak, David. "Buber and Tillich." *Journal of Ecumenical Studies*, Spring 1992:159–174.

Novak, Michael. "The Religion of Paul Tillich." *Commentary*, April 1967.

Noveck, Simon, ed. *Great Jewish Thinkers*. Washington, DC: B'nai B'rith Department of Adult Jewish Education, 1963.

Polner, Murray, and Naomi Goodman, eds. *The Challenge of Shalom: The Jewish Tradition of Peace and Justice.* Philadelphia: New Society Publishers, 1994.

Sherman, Franklin. *The Promise of Heschel.* Philadelphia: J.B. Lippincott, 1970.

Taylor, Mark Kline. *Paul Tillich: Theologian of the Boundaries.* London: Collins Liturgical Publications, 1987.

Tillich, Paul. *Biblical Religion and the Search for Ultimate Reality.* Chicago: University of Chicago Press, 1955.

———. *The Courage to Be.* New Haven: Yale University Press, 1952.

———. *Dynamics of Faith.* New York: Harper and Brothers, 1957.

———. *On the Boundary.* New York: Charles Scribner's Sons, 1966.

———. *Systematic Theology.* 3 vols. Chicago: University of Chicago Press, 1951–63.

CREDITS

Global Spiritual Perspectives

Spiritual Perspectives on America's Role as Superpower
by the Editors at SkyLight Paths

Are we the world's good neighbor or a global bully? From a spiritual perspec
what are America's responsibilities as the only remaining superpower? Contribu
**Dr. Beatrice Bruteau • Dr. Joan Brown Campbell • Tony Campolo • Rev. Forrest Churc
Lama Surya Das • Matthew Fox • Kabir Helminski • Thich Nhat Hanh • Eboo Patel • A
M. Basil Pennington, ocso • Dennis Prager • Rosemary Radford Ruether • Wayne Teasd
Rev. William McD. Tully • Rabbi Arthur Waskow • John Wilson**
5½ x 8½, 256 pp, Quality PB, 978-1-893361-81-2 **$16.95**

Spiritual Perspectives on Globalization, 2nd Edition
Making Sense of Economic and Cultural Upheaval
by Ira Rifkin; Foreword by Dr. David Little, Harvard Divinity School
What is globalization? Surveys the religious landscape. Includes a new Discu
Guide designed for group use.
5½ x 8½, 256 pp, Quality PB, 978-1-59473-045-0 **$16.99**

Hinduism / Vedanta

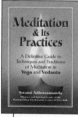

The Four Yogas
A Guide to the Spiritual Paths of Action, Devotion, Meditation and Knowledge
by Swami Adiswarananda 6 x 9, 320 pp, HC, 978-1-59473-143-3 **$29.99**

Meditation & Its Practices
A Definitive Guide to Techniques and Traditions of Meditation in Yoga and Vedanta
by Swami Adiswarananda 6 x 9, 504 pp, Quality PB, 978-1-59473-105-1 **$24.99**

The Spiritual Quest and the Way of Yoga: The Goal, the Journey and the Miles
by Swami Adiswarananda 6 x 9, 288 pp, HC, 978-1-59473-113-6 **$29.99**

Sri Ramakrishna, the Face of Silence
by Swami Nikhilananda and Dhan Gopal Mukerji
Edited with an Introduction by Swami Adiswarananda; Foreword by Dhan Gopal Mukerji II
Classic biographies present the life and thought of Sri Ramakrishna.
6 x 9, 352 pp, HC, 978-1-59473-115-0 **$29.99**

Sri Sarada Devi, The Holy Mother
Her Teachings and Conversations
Translated with Notes by Swami Nikhilananda; Edited with an Introduction by Swami Adiswara
6 x 9, 288 pp, HC, 978-1-59473-070-2 **$29.99**

The Vedanta Way to Peace and Happiness by Swami Adiswarananda
6 x 9, 240 pp, HC, 978-1-59473-034-4 **$29.99**

Vivekananda, World Teacher: His Teachings on the Spiritual Unity of Humanki
Edited and with an Introduction by Swami Adiswarananda
6 x 9, 272 pp, Quality PB, 978-1-59473-210-2 **$21.99**

Sikhism

The First Sikh Spiritual Master
Timeless Wisdom from the Life and Teachings of Guru Nanak by Harish D
Tells the story of a unique spiritual leader who showed a gentle, peaceful pa
God-realization while highlighting Guru Nanak's quest for tolerance and
passion. 6 x 9, 192 pp, Quality PB, 978-1-59473-209-6 **$16.99**

Meditation / Prayer

...yers to an Evolutionary God
...lliam Cleary; Afterword by Diarmuid O'Murchu
...w is it possible to pray when God is dislocated from heaven, dispersed all ...nd us, and more of a creative force than an all-knowing father? Inspired by ...spiritual and scientific teachings of Diarmuid O'Murchu and Teilhard de ...rdin, Cleary reveals that religion and science can be combined to create an ...nding view of the universe—an evolutionary faith.
208 pp, HC, 978-1-59473-006-1 **$21.99**

...lms: A Spiritual Commentary
Basil Pennington, OCSO; Illustrations by Phillip Ratner
...ving how the Psalms give profound and candid expression to both our high-...spirations and our deepest pain, the late, highly respected Cistercian Abbot ...asil Pennington shares his reflections on some of the most beloved passages ...the Bible's most widely read book.
176 pp, HC, 24 full-page b/w illus., 978-1-59473-141-9 **$19.99**

...e Song of Songs: A Spiritual Commentary
Basil Pennington, OCSO; Illustrations by Phillip Ratner
...the late M. Basil Pennington as he ruminates on the Bible's most challenging ...ical text. Follow a path into the Songs that weaves through his inspired ...ls and the evocative drawings of Jewish artist Phillip Ratner—a path that ...ls your own humanity and leads to the deepest delight of your soul.
160 pp, HC, 14 b/w illus., 978-1-59473-004-7 **$19.99**

...men of Color Pray: Voices of Strength, Faith, Healing,
...e and Courage *Edited and with Introductions by Christal M. Jackson*
...ugh these prayers, poetry, lyrics, meditations and affirmations, you will ...e in the strong and undeniable connection women of color share with God. ...ll challenge you to explore new ways of prayerful expression.
..., 208 pp, Quality PB, 978-1-59473-077-1 **$15.99**

...Art of Public Prayer: Not for Clergy Only
...vrence A. Hoffman
...cumenical resource for all people looking to change hardened worship patterns.
288 pp, Quality PB, 978-1-893361-06-5 **$18.99**

...ing Grace at the Center, 3rd Ed.: The Beginning of Centering Prayer
...Basil Pennington, OCSO, Thomas Keating, OCSO, and Thomas E. Clarke, SJ
...vord by Rev. Cynthia Bourgeault, PhD
...¾,128 pp, Quality PB, 978-1-59473-182-2 **$12.99**

...eart of Stillness: A Complete Guide to Learning the Art of Meditation
...avid A. Cooper 5½ x 8½, 272 pp, Quality PB, 978-1-893361-03-4 **$16.95**

...itation without Gurus: A Guide to the Heart of Practice
...ark Strand 5½ x 8½, 192 pp, Quality PB, 978-1-893361-93-5 **$16.95**

...ing with Our Hands: 21 Practices of Embodied Prayer from the World's
...tual Traditions *by Jon M. Sweeney; Photographs by Jennifer J. Wilson; Foreword by Mother ...Bielecki; Afterword by Taitetsu Unno, PhD*
..., 96 pp, 22 duotone photos, Quality PB, 978-1-893361-16-4 **$16.95**

...ce, Simplicity & Solitude: A Complete Guide to Spiritual Retreat at Home
...avid A. Cooper 5½ x 8½, 336 pp, Quality PB, 978-1-893361-04-1 **$16.95**

...e Gates to Meditation Practice: A Personal Journey into Sufism, Buddhism,
...Judaism *by David A. Cooper* 5½ x 8½, 240 pp, Quality PB, 978-1-893361-22-5 **$16.95**

...men Pray: Voices through the Ages, from Many Faiths, Cultures and Traditions
...d and with Introductions by Monica Furlong
...¾, 256 pp, Quality PB, 978-1-59473-071-9 **$15.99**
...xe HC with ribbon marker, 978-1-893361-25-6 **$19.95**

Spirituality

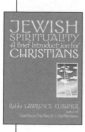

Jewish Spirituality: A Brief Introduction for Christians   *by Lawrence Kushner*
5½ x 8½, 112 pp, Quality PB, 978-1-58023-150-3 **$12.95** *(a Jewish Lights book)*

Journeys of Simplicity: Traveling Light with Thomas Merton, Bashō, Edward Abb
Annie Dillard & Others *by Philip Harnden* 5 x 7¼, 144 pp, Quality PB, 978-1-59473-181-5 **$1**
128 pp, HC, 978-1-893361-76-8 **$16.95**

Keeping Spiritual Balance As We Grow Older: More than 65 Creative Way
Use Purpose, Prayer, and the Power of Spirit to Build a Meaningful Retirement
by Molly and Bernie Srode 8 x 8, 224 pp, Quality PB, 978-1-59473-042-9 **$16.99**

The Monks of Mount Athos: A Western Monk's Extraordinary Spiritual Journey on
Eastern Holy Ground *by M. Basil Pennington, ocso; Foreword by Archimandrite Dionysios*
6 x 9, 256 pp, 10+ b/w line drawings, Quality PB, 978-1-893361-78-2 **$18.95**

One God Clapping: The Spiritual Path of a Zen Rabbi *by Alan Lew with Sherrill Jaff*
5½ x 8½, 336 pp, Quality PB, 978-1-58023-115-2 **$16.95** *(a Jewish Lights book)*

Prayer for People Who Think Too Much: A Guide to Everyday, Anywhere Pr
from the World's Faith Traditions *by Mitch Finley*
5½ x 8½, 224 pp, Quality PB, 978-1-893361-21-8 **$16.99**; HC, 978-1-893361-00-3 **$21.95**

Show Me Your Way: The Complete Guide to Exploring Interfaith Spiritual Direc
by Howard A. Addison 5½ x 8½, 240 pp, Quality PB, 978-1-893361-41-6 **$16.95**

Spirituality 101: The Indispensable Guide to Keeping—or Finding—Your Spiritua
on Campus *by Harriet L. Schwartz, with contributions from college students at nearly thirt*
campuses across the United States 6 x 9, 272 pp, Quality PB, 978-1-59473-000-9 **$16.99**

Spiritually Incorrect: Finding God in All the *Wrong* Places *by Dan Wakefield; Illus.*
Marian DelVecchio 5½ x 8½, 192 pp, b/w illus., Quality PB, 978-1-59473-137-2 **$15.99**

Spiritual Manifestos: Visions for Renewed Religious Life in America from Young
Spiritual Leaders of Many Faiths *Edited by Niles Elliot Goldstein; Preface by Martin E. Mar*
6 x 9, 256 pp, HC, 978-1-893361-09-6 **$21.95**

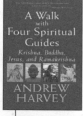

A Walk with Four Spiritual Guides: Krishna, Buddha, Jesus, and Ramakrishna
by Andrew Harvey 5½ x 8½, 192 pp, 10 b/w photos & illus.,Quality PB, 978-1-59473-138-9 **$1**

What Matters: Spiritual Nourishment for Head and Heart
by Frederick Franck 5 x 7¼, 128 pp, 50+ b/w illus., HC, 978-1-59473-013-9 **$16.99**

Who Is My God?, 2nd Edition: An Innovative Guide to Finding Your Spiritual Identit
Created by the Editors at SkyLight Paths 6 x 9, 160 pp, Quality PB, 978-1-59473-014-6 **$15.9**

Spirituality—A Week Inside

Come and Sit: A Week Inside Meditation Centers
by Marcia Z. Nelson; Foreword by Wayne Teasdale
The insider's guide to meditation in a variety of different spiritual traditio
Buddhist, Hindu, Christian, Jewish, and Sufi traditions.
6 x 9, 224 pp, b/w photos, Quality PB, 978-1-893361-35-5 **$16.95**

Lighting the Lamp of Wisdom: A Week Inside a Yoga Ashram
by John Ittner; Foreword by Dr. David Frawley
This insider's guide to Hindu spiritual life takes you into a typical week of r
inside a yoga ashram to demystify the experience and show you what to expe
6 x 9, 192 pp, 10+ b/w photos, Quality PB, 978-1-893361-52-2 **$15.95**

Making a Heart for God: A Week Inside a Catholic Monastery
by Dianne Aprile; Foreword by Brother Patrick Hart, ocso
Takes you to the Abbey of Gethsemani—the Trappist monastery in Kent
that was home to author Thomas Merton—to explore the details.
6 x 9, 224 pp, b/w photos, Quality PB, 978-1-893361-49-2 **$16.95**

Waking Up: A Week Inside a Zen Monastery
by Jack Maguire; Foreword by John Daido Loori, Roshi
An essential guide to what it's like to spend a week inside a Zen Buddhist mona
6 x 9, 224 pp, b/w photos, Quality PB, 978-1-893361-55-3 **$16.95**
HC, 978-1-893361-13-3 **$21.95**

Kabbalah from Jewish Lights Publishing

kening to Kabbalah: The Guiding Light of Spiritual Fulfillment
ıv Michael Laitman, PhD 6 x 9, 192 pp, HC, 978-1-58023-264-7 **$21.99**

in God's Image: Discover Your Personality Type Using the Enneagram and Kabbalah
ıbbi Howard A. Addison 7 x 9, 176 pp, Quality PB, 978-1-58023-124-4 **$16.95**

ıh: A Kabbalah for Tomorrow by Dr. Arthur Green
', 224 pp, Quality PB, 978-1-58023-213-5 **$16.99**

Enneagram and Kabbalah, 2nd Edition: Reading Your Soul
ıbbi Howard A. Addison 6 x 9, 192 pp, Quality PB, 978-1-58023-229-6 **$16.99**

ing Joy: A Practical Spiritual Guide to Happiness by Dannel I. Schwartz with Mark Hass
, 192 pp, Quality PB, 978-1-58023-009-4 **$14.95**

Gift of Kabbalah: Discovering the Secrets of Heaven, Renewing Your Life on Earth
ınar Frankiel, PhD 6 x 9, 256 pp, Quality PB, 978-1-58023-141-1 **$16.95**
)78-1-58023-108-4 **$21.95**

ey from the Rock: An Easy Introduction to Jewish Mysticism
ıwrence Kushner 6 x 9, 176 pp, Quality PB, 978-1-58023-073-5 **$16.95**

ıalah: A Brief Introduction for Christians
ınar Frankiel, PhD 5½ x 8½, 176 pp, Quality PB, 978-1-58023-303-3 **$16.99**

ır: Annotated & Explained Translation and Annotation by Dr. Daniel C. Matt
ıord by Andrew Harvey 5½ x 8½, 176 pp, Quality PB, 978-1-893361-51-5 **$15.99**

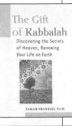

Judaism / Christianity

ıstians and Jews in Dialogue: Learning in the Presence of the Other
ıry C. Boys and Sara S. Lee; Foreword by Dorothy C. Bass
ıres renewed commitment to dialogue between religious traditions and illu-
ıes how it should happen. Explains the transformative work of creating envi-
ıents for Jews and Christians to study together and enter the dynamism of
ıther's religious tradition.
, 240 pp, HC, 978-1-59473-144-0 **$21.99**

ıing the Jewish-Christian Rift: Growing Beyond Our Wounded History
ın Miller and Laura Bernstein; Foreword by Dr. Beatrice Bruteau
, 288 pp, Quality PB, 978-1-59473-139-6 **$18.99**

ıducing My Faith and My Community
ıwish Outreach Institute Guide for the Christian in a Jewish Interfaith Relationship
ıbbi Kerry M. Olitzky 6 x 9, 176 pp, Quality PB, 978-1-58023-192-3 **$16.99** (a Jewish Lights book)

ıewish Approach to God: A Brief Introduction for Christians
ıbbi Neil Gillman 5½ x 8½, 192 pp, Quality PB, 978-1-58023-190-9 **$16.95** (a Jewish Lights book)

ıh Holidays: A Brief Introduction for Christians
ıbbi Kerry M. Olitzky and Rabbi Daniel Judson
ı8½, 176 pp, Quality PB, 978-1-58023-302-6 **$16.99** (a Jewish Lights book)

ıh Ritual: A Brief Introduction for Christians
ıbbi Kerry M. Olitzky and Rabbi Daniel Judson
ı8½, 144 pp, Quality PB, 978-1-58023-210-4 **$14.99** (a Jewish Lights book)

ıh Spirituality: A Brief Introduction for Christians
ıbbi Lawrence Kushner
ı8½, 112 pp, Quality PB, 978-1-58023-150-3 **$12.95** (a Jewish Lights book)

ıvish Understanding of the New Testament
ıbbi Samuel Sandmel; new Preface by Rabbi David Sandmel
ı8½, 368 pp, Quality PB, 978-1-59473-048-1 **$19.99**

Jews and Jesus
ıring Theological Differences for Mutual Understanding
ıbi Samuel Sandmel; new Preface by Rabbi David Sandmel A Classic Reprint
ıen in a non-technical way for the layperson, this candid and forthright look
ı what and why of the Jewish attitude toward Jesus is a clear and forceful
ısition that guides both Christians and Jews in relevant discussion.
ı 92 pp, Quality PB, 978-1-59473-208-9 **$16.99**

Spirituality & Crafts

The Knitting Way: A Guide to Spiritual Self-Discovery
by Linda Skolnik and Janice MacDaniels
7 x 9, 240 pp, Quality PB, b/w photographs, 978-1-59473-079-5 **$16.99**

The Quilting Path: A Guide to Spiritual Discovery through Fabric, Thread and Kab
by Louise Silk
7 x 9, 192 pp, Quality PB, b/w photographs and illustrations, 978-1-59473-206-5 **$16.9**

The Scrapbooking Journey: A Hands-On Guide to Spiritual Discovery
by Cory Richardson-Lauve; Foreword by Stacy Julian
7 x 9, 176 pp, Quality PB, 8-page full-color insert, plus b/w photographs
978-1-59473-216-4 **$18.99**

Spiritual Practice

Divining the Body: Reclaim the Holiness of Your Physical Self
by Jan Phillips
A practical and inspiring guidebook for connecting the body and soul in spi
practice. Leads you into a milieu of reverence, mystery and delight, helping
discover your body as a pathway to the Divine.
8 x 8, 256 pp, Quality PB, 978-1-59473-080-1 **$16.99**

Finding Time for the Timeless: Spirituality in the Workweek
by John McQuiston II
Simple, refreshing stories that provide you with examples of how you can
cus and enrich your daily life using prayer or meditation, ritual and other
of spiritual practice. 5½ x 6¾, 208 pp, HC, 978-1-59473-035-1 **$17.99**

The Gospel of Thomas: A Guidebook for Spiritual Practice
by Ron Miller; Translations by Stevan Davies
An innovative guide to bring a new spiritual classic into daily life.
6 x 9, 160 pp, Quality PB, 978-1-59473-047-4 **$14.99**

Earth, Water, Fire, and Air: Essential Ways of Connecting to Spirit
by Cait Johnson 6 x 9, 224 pp, HC, 978-1-893361-65-2 **$19.95**

Labyrinths from the Outside In: Walking to Spiritual Insight—A Beginner's G
by Donna Schaper and Carole Ann Camp
6 x 9, 208 pp, b/w illus. and photos, Quality PB, 978-1-893361-18-8 **$16.95**

Practicing the Sacred Art of Listening: A Guide to Enrich Your Relationshi
and Kindle Your Spiritual Life—The Listening Center Workshop
by Kay Lindahl 8 x 8, 176 pp, Quality PB, 978-1-893361-85-0 **$16.95**

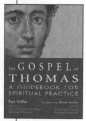

Releasing the Creative Spirit: Unleash the Creativity in Your Life
by Dan Wakefield 7 x 10, 256 pp, Quality PB, 978-1-893361-36-2 **$16.95**

The Sacred Art of Bowing: Preparing to Practice
by Andi Young 5½ x 8½, 128 pp, b/w illus., Quality PB, 978-1-893361-82-9 **$14.95**

The Sacred Art of Chant: Preparing to Practice
by Ana Hernández 5½ x 8½, 192 pp, Quality PB, 978-1-59473-036-8 **$15.99**

The Sacred Art of Fasting: Preparing to Practice
by Thomas Ryan, CSP 5½ x 8½, 192 pp, Quality PB, 978-1-59473-078-8 **$15.99**

The Sacred Art of Forgiveness: Forgiving Ourselves and Others through God's
by Marcia Ford 8 x 8, 176 pp, Quality PB, 978-1-59473-175-4 **$16.99**

The Sacred Art of Listening: Forty Reflections for Cultivating a Spiritual Pract
by Kay Lindahl; Illustrations by Amy Schnapper
8 x 8, 160 pp, b/w illus., Quality PB, 978-1-893361-44-7 **$16.99**

The Sacred Art of Lovingkindness: Preparing to Practice
by Rabbi Rami Shapiro; Foreword by Marcia Ford
5½ x 8½, 176 pp, Quality PB, 978-1-59473-151-8 **$16.99**

Sacred Speech: A Practical Guide for Keeping Spirit in Your Speech
by Rev. Donna Schaper 6 x 9, 176 pp, Quality PB, 978-1-59473-068-9 **$15.99**
HC, 978-1-893361-74-4 **$21.95**

Spirituality of the Seasons

...umn: A Spiritual Biography of the Season
by Gary Schmidt and Susan M. Felch; Illustrations by Mary Azarian
...ce in autumn as a time of preparation and reflection. Includes Wendell Berry,
...l James Duncan, Robert Frost, A. Bartlett Giamatti, E. B. White, P. D. James,
...t of Norwich, Garret Keizer, Tracy Kidder, Anne Lamott, May Sarton.
...320 pp, 5 b/w illus., Quality PB, 978-1-59473-118-1 **$18.99**
...78-1-59473-005-4 **$22.99**

...ng: A Spiritual Biography of the Season
by Gary Schmidt and Susan M. Felch; Illustrations by Mary Azarian
...re the gentle unfurling of spring and reflect on how nature celebrates rebirth
...renewal. Includes Jane Kenyon, Lucy Larcom, Harry Thurston, Nathaniel
...horne, Noel Perrin, Annie Dillard, Martha Ballard, Barbara Kingsolver,
...thy Wordsworth, Donald Hall, David Brill, Lionel Basney, Isak Dinesen, Paul
...nce Dunbar. 6 x 9, 352 pp, 6 b/w illus., HC, 978-1-59473-114-3 **$21.99**

...mer: A Spiritual Biography of the Season
by Gary Schmidt and Susan M. Felch; Illustrations by Barry Moser
...mptuous banquet.... These selections lift up an exquisite wholeness found
...n an everyday sophistication."— ★ *Publishers Weekly* starred review
...les Anne Lamott, Luci Shaw, Ray Bradbury, Richard Selzer, Thomas Lynch,
...Whitman, Carl Sandburg, Sherman Alexie, Madeleine L'Engle, Jamaica Kincaid.
...04 pp, 5 b/w illus., Quality PB, 978-1-59473-183-9 **$18.99**
...8-1-59473-083-2 **$21.99**

...ter: A Spiritual Biography of the Season
by Gary Schmidt and Susan M. Felch; Illustrations by Barry Moser
...outstanding anthology features top-flight nature and spirituality writers on
...rce, inexorable season of winter.... Remarkably lively and warm, despite the
...bject." — ★ *Publishers Weekly* starred review.
...es Will Campbell, Rachel Carson, Annie Dillard, Donald Hall, Ron Hansen, Jane
...n, Jamaica Kincaid, Barry Lopez, Kathleen Norris, John Updike, E. B. White.
...288 pp, 6 b/w illus., Deluxe PB w/flaps, 978-1-893361-92-8 **$18.95**
...78-1-893361-53-9 **$21.95**

Spirituality / Animal Companions

...ing the Animals: Prayers and Ceremonies to Celebrate God's Creatures, Wild
...ame *Edited by Lynn L. Caruso* 5 x 7¼, 256 pp, HC, 978-1-59473-145-7 **$19.99**

...t Animals Can Teach Us about Spirituality: Inspiring Lessons from Wild and
...Creatures *by Diana L. Guerrero* 6 x 9, 176 pp, Quality PB, 978-1-893361-84-3 **$16.95**

Spirituality

...kening the Spirit, Inspiring the Soul
...ories of Interspiritual Discovery in the Community of Faiths
...*by Brother Wayne Teasdale and Martha Howard, MD; Foreword by Joan Borysenko, PhD*
...r original spiritual mini-autobiographies showcase the varied ways that
...e come to faith—and what that means—in today's multi-religious world.
...24 pp, HC, 978-1-59473-039-9 **$21.99**

...Alphabet of Paradise: An A–Z of Spirituality for Everyday Life
...ward Cooper 5 x 7¾, 224 pp, Quality PB, 978-1-893361-80-5 **$16.95**

...ting a Spiritual Retirement: A Guide to the Unseen Possibilities in Our Lives
...lly Srode 6 x 9, 208 pp, b/w photos, Quality PB, 978-1-59473-050-4 **$14.99**
...78-1-893361-75-1 **$19.95**

...ng Hope: Cultivating God's Gift of a Hopeful Spirit
...rcia Ford 8 x 8, 200 pp, Quality PB, 978-1-59473-211-9 **$16.99**

...Geography of Faith: Underground Conversations on Religious, Political and Social
...ge *by Daniel Berrigan and Robert Coles* 6 x 9, 224 pp, Quality PB, 978-1-893361-40-9 **$16.95**

...Within: Our Spiritual Future—As Told by Today's New Adults *Edited by Jon M. Sweeney*
...e Editors at SkyLight Paths 6 x 9, 176 pp, Quality PB, 978-1-893361-15-7 **$14.95**

Sacred Texts—SkyLight Illuminations Seri

Offers today's spiritual seeker an accessible entry into the great classic texts of world's spiritual traditions. Each classic is presented in an accessible transla with facing pages of guided commentary from experts, giving you the key need to understand the history, context and meaning of the text. This enables you, whatever your background, to experience and understand c spiritual texts directly, and to make them a part of your life.

CHRISTIANITY

The End of Days: Essential Selections from Apocalyptic Texts— Annotated & Explained *Annotation by Robert G. Clouse*
Helps you understand the complex Christian visions of the end of the world.
5½ x 8½, 224 pp, Quality PB, 978-1-59473-170-9 **$16.99**

The Hidden Gospel of Matthew: Annotated & Explained
Translation & Annotation by Ron Miller
Takes you deep into the text cherished around the world to discover the v and events that have the strongest connection to the historical Jesus.
5½ x 8½, 272 pp, Quality PB, 978-1-59473-038-2 **$16.99**

The Lost Sayings of Jesus: Teachings from Ancient Christian, Jewis Gnostic and Islamic Sources—Annotated & Explained
Translation & Annotation by Andrew Phillip Smith; Foreword by Stephan A. Hoeller
This collection of more than three hundred sayings depicts Jesus as a Wi teacher who speaks to people of all faiths as a mystic and spiritual master.
5½ x 8½, 240 pp, Quality PB, 978-1-59473-172-3 **$16.99**

Philokalia: The Eastern Christian Spiritual Texts—Selections Annotat Explained *Annotation by Allyne Smith; Translation by G. E. H. Palmer, Phillip Sherrard Bishop Kallistos Ware*
The first approachable introduction to the wisdom of the Philokalia, which classic text of Eastern Christian spirituality.
5½ x 8½, 240 pp, Quality PB, 978-1-59473-103-7 **$16.99**

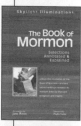

Spiritual Writings on Mary: Annotated & Explained
Annotation by Mary Ford-Grabowsky; Foreword by Andrew Harvey
Examines the role of Mary, the mother of Jesus, as a source of inspiration i history and in life today. 5½ x 8½, 288 pp, Quality PB, 978-1-59473-001-6 **$16.99**

The Way of a Pilgrim: The Jesus Prayer Journey—Annotated & Expla
Translation & Annotation by Gleb Pokrovsky; Foreword by Andrew Harvey
This classic of Russian spirituality is the delightful account of one man wh out to learn the prayer of the heart, also known as the "Jesus prayer."
5½ x 8½, 160 pp, Illus., Quality PB, 978-1-893361-31-7 **$14.95**

MORMONISM

The Book of Mormon: Selections Annotated & Explained
Annotation by Jana Riess; Foreword by Phyllis Tickle
Explores the sacred epic that is cherished by more than twelve million me of the LDS church as the keystone of their faith.
5½ x 8½ , 272 pp, Quality PB, 978-1-59473-076-4 **$16.99**

NATIVE AMERICAN

Native American Stories of the Sacred: Annotated & Explained
Retold & Annotated by Evan T. Pritchard
Intended for more than entertainment, these teaching tales contain elegantl ple illustrations of time-honored truths.
5½ x 8½, 272 pp, Quality PB, 978-1-59473-112-9 **$16.99**

Sacred Texts—cont.

GNOSTICISM

Gospel of Philip: Annotated & Explained
ation & Annotation by Andrew Phillip Smith; Foreword by Stevan Davies
als otherwise unrecorded sayings of Jesus and fragments of Gnostic mythology.
3½, 160 pp, Quality PB, 978-1-59473-111-2 **$16.99**

Gospel of Thomas: Annotated & Explained
ation & Annotation by Stevan Davies Sheds new light on the origins of Christianity and
ays Jesus as a wisdom-loving sage. 5½ x 8½, 192 pp, Quality PB, 978-1-893361-45-4 **$16.99**

Secret Book of John: The Gnostic Gospel—Annotated & Explained
ation & Annotation by Stevan Davies The most significant and influential text of
ancient Gnostic religion. 5½ x 8½, 208 pp, Quality PB, 978-1-59473-082-5 **$16.99**

JUDAISM

Divine Feminine in Biblical Wisdom Literature
tions Annotated & Explained
ation & Annotation by Rabbi Rami Shapiro; Foreword by Rev. Cynthia Bourgeault, PhD
the Hebrew books of Psalms, Proverbs, Song of Songs, Ecclesiastes and Job,
om literature and the Wisdom of Solomon to clarify who Wisdom is.
½, 240 pp, Quality PB, 978-1-59473-109-9 **$16.99**

cs of the Sages: *Pirke Avot*—Annotated & Explained
ation & Annotation by Rabbi Rami Shapiro Clarifies the ethical teachings of the
Rabbis. 5½ x 8½, 192 pp, Quality PB, 978-1-59473-207-2 **$16.99**

idic Tales: Annotated & Explained
ation & Annotation by Rabbi Rami Shapiro
luces the legendary tales of the impassioned Hasidic rabbis, presenting them as
s rather than as parables. 5½ x 8½, 240 pp, Quality PB, 978-1-893361-86-7 **$16.95**

Hebrew Prophets: Selections Annotated & Explained
ation & Annotation by Rabbi Rami Shapiro; Foreword by Zalman M. Schachter-Shalomi
es on the central themes covered by all the Hebrew prophets.
½, 224 pp, Quality PB, 978-1-59473-037-5 **$16.99**

ar: Annotated & Explained *Translation & Annotation by Daniel C. Matt*
est-selling author of *The Essential Kabbalah* brings together in one place the most
tant teachings of the Zohar, the canonical text of Jewish mystical tradition.
½, 176 pp, Quality PB, 978-1-893361-51-5 **$15.99**

EASTERN RELIGIONS

gavad Gita: Annotated & Explained *Translation by Shri Purohit Swami*
tion by Kendra Crossen Burroughs* Explains references and philosophical terms,
s the interpretations of famous spiritual leaders and scholars, and more.
½, 192 pp, Quality PB, 978-1-893361-28-7 **$16.95**

nmapada: Annotated & Explained *Translation by Max Müller and revised by
aguire; Annotation by Jack Maguire* Contains all of Buddhism's key teachings.
½, 160 pp, b/w photos, Quality PB, 978-1-893361-42-3 **$14.95**

i and Islam: Selections from His Stories, Poems, and Discourses—
tated & Explained *Translation & Annotation by Ibrahim Gamard*
es on Rumi's place within the Sufi tradition of Islam, providing insight into
ystical side of the religion. 5½ x 8½, 240 pp, Quality PB, 978-1-59473-002-3 **$15.99**

tions from the Gospel of Sri Ramakrishna: Annotated & Explained
tion by Swami Nikhilananda; Annotation by Kendra Crossen Burroughs
luces the fascinating world of the Indian mystic and the universal appeal
message. 5½ x 8½, 240 pp, b/w photos, Quality PB, 978-1-893361-46-1 **$16.95**

e Ching: Annotated & Explained *Translation & Annotation by Derek Lin*
rd by Lama Surya Das* Introduces an Eastern classic in an accessible, poetic
mpletely original way. 5½ x 8½, 192 pp, Quality PB, 978-1-59473-204-1 **$16.99**

About SKYLIGHT PATHS Publishing

SkyLight Paths Publishing is creating a place where people of differ
spiritual traditions come together for challenge and inspiration, a pl
where we can help each other understand the mystery that lies at the he
of our existence.

Through spirituality, our religious beliefs are increasingly becoming a par
our lives—rather than *apart* from our lives. While many of us may be m
interested than ever in spiritual growth, we may be less firmly planted in
ditional religion. Yet, we do want to deepen our relationship to the sacred
learn from our own as well as from other faith traditions, and to practic
new ways.

SkyLight Paths sees both believers and seekers as a community that incr
ingly transcends traditional boundaries of religion and denomination—pe
wanting to learn from each other, *walking together, finding the way.*

For your information and convenience, at the back of this book we h
provided a list of other SkyLight Paths books you might find interes
and useful. They cover the following subjects:

Buddhism / Zen	Gnosticism	Mysticism
Catholicism	Hinduism /	Poetry
Children's Books	Vedanta	Prayer
Christianity	Inspiration	Religious Etiquette
Comparative	Islam / Sufism	Retirement
Religion	Judaism / Kabbalah /	Spiritual Biography
Current Events	Enneagram	Spiritual Direction
Earth-Based	Meditation	Spirituality
Spirituality	Midrash Fiction	Women's Interest
Global Spiritual	Monasticism	Worship
Perspectives		